the modernfamily™
cookbook

the

modern family™

cookbook

 MELCHER MEDIA Oxmoor House®

meet the chefs

claire

FAVORITE RECIPE:
Arugula Salad with Prosciutto
and Pears, p. 84

"My kids are
middle-management
material at best."

phil

FAVORITE RECIPE:
Multigrain Malt Waffles, p. 24

"When life gives you
lemonade, make lemons.
Life will be all like,
'What?!?!'"

luke

FAVORITE RECIPE:
Doughnut Waffle Sundaes,
p. 200

"For the record, I do
all my own wiping."

alex

FAVORITE RECIPE:
Fresh Fruit Salad
with Lime-Ginger
Syrup, p. 28

"Grandpa is
my friend."

haley

FAVORITE RECIPE:
Killer Margs, p. 228

"With great
hotness
comes great
responsibility."

Some say that too many cooks spoil the broth, but not in the Dunphy-Tucker-Pritchett-Delgado clan. They have big personalities and even bigger appetites. Here's your chance to get to know the chefs who are dishing out the recipes throughout this book, so pull up a chair and get ready to *Phil* your plate!

THE PRITCHETT-DELGADOS

gloria
FAVORITE RECIPE:
Carnitas al Diablo, p. 160

"I know you can't tell by looking at me, but I'm not a natural homemaker."

jay
FAVORITE RECIPE:
Grilled Beef Tenderloin with Chimichurri, p. 140

"Nobody doesn't like me. I'm Jay. I'm salt of the earth."

manny
FAVORITE RECIPE:
French Toast Sticks, p. 30

"I've always felt out of place in public school, like a long petunia in an onion patch."

joe
FAVORITE RECIPE:
Fruit-Yogurt Pops, p. 48

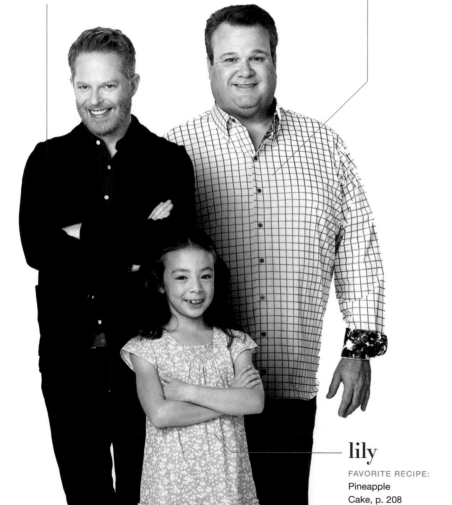

mitchell

FAVORITE RECIPE:
Vegetable-Gruyère Quiche, p. 36

"I haven't been judged by this many people since I forgot my canvas bags at Whole Foods."

cam

FAVORITE RECIPE:
PB & J Tartines, p. 100

"Prepare to feel like an old denim vest because I'm about to be-dazzling you."

lily

FAVORITE RECIPE:
Pineapple
Cake, p. 208

"You guys exhaust me."

cam's grandmother's housekeeper delilah

FAVORITE RECIPE: Biscuits and Gravy, p. 39

pepper

(Cam and Mitchell's friend)

FAVORITE RECIPE: Citrus, Fennel, and Rosemary Olives, p. 71

skip woosnum

(Phil's colleague)

FAVORITE RECIPE: Wedge Salad, p. 82

jay's mother

FAVORITE RECIPE: Tomato Sauce with Spaghetti, p.137

lorraine

(Phil's client)

FAVORITE RECIPE: Zucchini Bread, p. 190

diane

(Phil's client)

FAVORITE RECIPE: Corn Bread, p. 192

andy

(Jay and Gloria's "manny")

FAVORITE RECIPE: Flaxseed Muffins, p. 193

kelly

(Manny's former girlfriend)

FAVORITE RECIPE: Salted Chocolate Milk, p. 230

dede

(Jay's ex-wife)

FAVORITE RECIPE: Horny Colombian Cocktails, p. 235

make yourself
at home

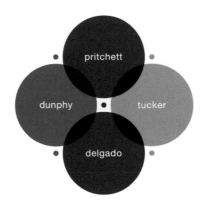

The best way to really get to know someone is to take a tour of their home. The unique personalities of the Dunphy, Pritchett-Delgado, and Tucker-Pritchett families are reflected in their decorating choices. This handy guide offers tips for achieving each family's singular style. It also serves as a primer for the rest of the book. The recipes throughout are color-coded to match the palette of each family's home decor, so to choose meals from a specific family's arsenal of recipes, just look out for their corresponding colors on the pages ahead.

❖

Sunny Comfort

You don't get be the Two-Time Nonconsecutive District Realtor of the Year™ without knowing a thing or two about what turns a house into an enviable home. That's why Phil and Claire's updated-Craftsman-style house is warm and comfortable from top to bottom. Their kitchen serves as the hub of Dunphy Central, and it opens up into the dining and informal living rooms. The entire family can cook, do homework, and play video games within easy view of one another.

The Dunphys' walls boast bright, bold colors, while the furniture and woodwork combine neutrals to balance the aesthetic (blond-stained kitchen cabinets, an off-white dining table and chairs, and a plush couch). Claire and Phil also love their stripes. From throw pillows to table runners to rugs, the vertical and horizontal lines in the Dunphy house add simple texture to their living space.

Sleek Luxury

The Pritchett-Delgados' chic, ultramodern home fits Gloria's personality perfectly. Dark red accents; bright, floral artwork; and the occasional zebra pattern spice up their all-white kitchen. As a high-end closet-systems mogul, Jay has a stable of top craftspeople to call on for remodeling work, and it shows in the open-plan kitchen, breakfast area, and dining room.

Creamy custom cabinetry is set off with frosted-glass doors. The appliances are top-of-the-line and include a built-in wine fridge and plenty of stainless steel. The dark lacquered wood dining table offers plenty of seating for the grown-ups, while a glass-topped table with stainless-steel-framed chairs (not pictured here) serves as a dining area for the kids. (And occasionally for Jay's sons-in-law, when they make him angry.)

Asian Fusion

Nobody hosts a cocktail hour like Cam and Mitchell, not even Pepper Saltzman. Half of their party-throwing success is down to Cam's commitment to party themes; the other half is their trendy, elegant home. Cam and Mitchell's 1920s Spanish-Mediterranean-style duplex finds the perfect balance between contemporary and traditional.

Striking, adventurous artwork contrasts nicely with the muted green walls in the living room. Straight-lined, Asian-inspired furniture in muted grays is simple but stylish. Their cozy kitchen is butter yellow, with cream cabinets and gray tile countertops. Their house isn't as open as Claire and Phil's or Gloria and Jay's, but a wall cutout provides easy access between the kitchen and the living room, making it easy for Cam and Mitchell to pass cocktails, and covert judgments on their guests, back and forth between the two rooms.

BREAKFAST

the dunphys' | cornmeal-buttermilk pancakes

Season 2, Episode 11

CLAIRE:

What is the one thing a speeder can't outrun?

LUKE:

Oooh, bullets? A laser? Oh, I know, a falcon? Dad, jump in.

PHIL:

Not a good time.

LUKE:

A laser-falcon?

PHIL:

That's awesome.

Makes about 8 (4-inch) pancakes

1½ cups homemade pancake mix (see Note)

1 large egg

1 cup buttermilk

1 tablespoon vegetable oil

Unsalted butter

Syrup (optional)

1 Put the pancake mix in a medium bowl and add the egg, buttermilk, and oil. Beat, using a wire whisk, until blended.

2 For each pancake, pour ¼ cup batter onto a hot, lightly buttered griddle. Cook until the tops of the pancakes are covered with bubbles and the edges appear slightly dry. Turn and continue cooking until the bottoms are browned. Serve hot, with syrup if you like.

NOTE: To make enough pancake mix for four batches, in a large bowl, combine 4 cups all-purpose flour, ¾ cup yellow cornmeal, ½ cup brown sugar, ¼ cup baking powder, 2 teaspoons baking soda, and 2 teaspoons kosher salt. Spoon the mixture into a heavy-duty zip-top bag or an airtight container. Store in a cool cupboard or in the freezer for up to 3 months.

phil's | traditional first-day-of-school pancakes

Makes about 6 (8-inch) pancakes

2 cups all-purpose flour

2 tablespoons sugar

4 teaspoons baking powder

½ teaspoon kosher salt

1⅓ cups milk

1 large egg, beaten

2 tablespoons unsalted butter or margarine, melted, plus more for the griddle and serving

Syrup and whipped cream topping

1 Combine the flour, sugar, baking powder, and salt in a large mixing bowl. Combine the milk and egg in a separate bowl, mixing well; slowly stir into the dry ingredients. Gradually add the butter to the batter, stirring well.

2 For each pancake, pour ½ cup batter onto a hot, lightly buttered griddle. Cook until the tops of the pancakes are covered with bubbles and the edges appear slightly dry. Turn and continue cooking until the bottoms are browned. Serve with butter and syrup, and squirt a whipped-cream smiley face onto each pancake.

Season 1, Episode 1

PHIL:
I'm the cool dad. That's—that's my thing. I'm hip. I-I surf the Web, I text: LOL—Laugh out loud; OMG—Oh, my God; WTF—Why the face. Um, you know, I know all the dances to *High School Musical* . . .

"Traditional 'first-day-of-school' pancakes. Whipped-cream smile?"

—PHIL

claire's | fudgy chocolate chip pancakes

Makes about 9 (4-inch) pancakes

1 cup all-purpose flour

¼ cup cocoa powder

2 tablespoons sugar

1 teaspoon baking powder

¼ teaspoon baking soda

⅛ teaspoon kosher salt

1 cup buttermilk

1 tablespoon vegetable oil

1 large egg, lightly beaten

⅓ cup semisweet chocolate chips

Cooking spray

Hot fudge topping, whipped cream topping, raspberries

1 Combine the flour, cocoa powder, sugar, baking powder, baking soda, and salt in a large bowl; stir with a whisk. Combine the buttermilk, oil, and egg in a separate bowl; add to the flour mixture, stirring until well blended. Stir in the chocolate chips.

2 For each pancake, pour ¼ cup batter onto a medium-hot griddle lightly coated with cooking spray (the chocolate will burn if the pan is too hot). Cook until the tops of the pancakes are covered with bubbles and the edges appear slightly dry. Turn and continue cooking until the bottoms are browned.

3 Microwave the hot fudge topping according to the package directions. Serve the pancakes with fudge topping, whipped cream topping, and raspberries.

Season 4, Episode 10

CLAIRE:

Haley! Hurry up. You don't have much time, and I made chocolate chip pancakes.

HALEY:

Mom, I'm not 12.

PHIL:

Dibs on hers. Honey, you excited about your first day?

HALEY:

You know what? I really am. There's something about going to work that makes you feel like you're—I don't know— worth something. No offense, Mom.

phil's | multigrain malt waffle

Makes about 5 waffles

Cooking spray

1 cup plus 2 tablespoons homemade multigrain malt waffle mix (see Note)

⅔ cup milk

2 tablespoons toasted walnut oil

1 teaspoon vanilla extract

1 large egg

Confectioners' sugar (optional)

1 Coat a waffle iron with cooking spray; preheat.

2 Put the waffle mix in a bowl. Combine the milk, oil, vanilla, and egg in a separate bowl, stirring well with a whisk; add to the waffle mix, stirring well. Let the batter stand for 5 minutes.

3 Spoon about ⅓ cup batter per 4-inch waffle onto the hot waffle iron, spreading the batter to the edges. Cook for 5 minutes or until the steaming stops; repeat with the remaining batter. Garnish with confectioners' sugar if desired.

NOTE: To make enough waffle mix for about six batches, in a large bowl, combine 2½ cups all-purpose flour, 2 cups whole-wheat flour, 6 tablespoons spelt flour, 1 cup yellow cornmeal, ½ cup sugar, ½ cup malted milk powder, 3 tablespoons baking powder, 2 tablespoons toasted wheat germ, and 1 tablespoon kosher salt. Store in an airtight container in the refrigerator for up to 3 months.

TIP: Make these healthy waffles even more delicious by topping them with a spoonful of Alex's Fresh Fruit Salad with Lime-Ginger Syrup (page 28).

See photo on following spread

Season 6, Episode 11

PHIL, AFTER NARROWLY AVOIDING A CAR ACCIDENT:

Everybody calm down. Calm down. Let's not overreact.

CLAIRE:

What?!

HALEY:

Dad! We were almost just killed!

PHIL:

Exactly. Almost, which means we're all just fine.

CLAIRE:

You aren't the least bit upset?

PHIL:

It's gonna take more than that to ruin a morning that started with a whipped-cream smile on my waffle.

alex's | green tea–kiwi *and* mango smoothie

Makes about 4 cups; serves 4

2½ cups frozen diced mango (or about 2 large ripe mangoes)

¾ cup low-fat or fat-free vanilla yogurt

4 tablespoons honey

½ teaspoon grated lime zest

3 ripe kiwifruit, peeled and quartered, plus slices for serving

2 cups ice cubes

½ cup packed baby spinach

2 tablespoons bottled green tea

1 Put the mango, ½ cup of the yogurt, 2 tablespoons of the honey, 2 tablespoons water, and the lime zest in a blender; process until smooth, stirring occasionally. Divide among four glasses; place the glasses in the freezer.

2 Rinse the blender container. Put the remaining ¼ cup yogurt and 2 tablespoons honey, the quartered kiwifruit, ice, spinach, and tea in the blender; process until smooth, stirring occasionally. Gently spoon the kiwi mixture onto the mango mixture in the glasses, working carefully around the inside of each glass to create a clean horizontal line. Garnish with kiwifruit slices, if desired, and serve immediately.

TIP: You can save time by measuring out the ingredients for the kiwi-spinach layer and putting it all in a sealable container in the fridge the night before.

See photo on following spread

Season 2, Episode 16

HALEY, PRETENDING TO BE A WAITRESS TO TRICK HER PARENTS INTO HELPING HER PAY FOR A NEW CAR:
Ah, so your table is right here.

CLAIRE:
Oh, honey, would you mind getting us a couple drinks. I would love an iced tea.

PHIL:
Same, please.

ALEX:
I'll have a mango-kiwi smoothie, yogurt instead of ice cream, and make it low-fat—I wanna look good when I'm riding in your new car.

HALEY, AFTER OVERHEARING
ALEX PRACTICE HER SPEECH:

What?! Is that your speech?

ALEX:

Get out of here!

HALEY:

You cannot say that!

ALEX:

Yes, I can, and you want
to know why? 'Cause it's
the truth.

HALEY:

No one wants to hear the
truth! It's very simple, Alex.
In order to give a good
speech, all you have to do
is take a song and say it.
Like, "Don't Stop
Believin'" or "Get This
Party Started."

alex's | fresh fruit salad *with* lime-ginger syrup

Makes about 4 cups; serves 8

⅓ cup fresh lime juice

¼ cup fresh orange juice

2 tablespoons sugar

2 tablespoons honey

¼ teaspoon ground ginger

1 teaspoon grated lime zest

1 teaspoon grated orange zest

1½ cups cubed pineapple

1½ cups cubed peeled ripe mango
(about 2 small)

½ cup blueberries

2 kiwifruit, peeled and cubed

1 Combine the lime juice, orange juice, ⅓ cup water, the sugar, honey, and ginger in a small saucepan. Bring to a boil over medium heat; cook, whisking constantly, for 5 minutes or until reduced to ½ cup. Remove from the heat; let cool. Stir in the lime and orange zests.

2 Combine the pineapple, mango, blueberries, and kiwi in a large bowl. Pour the syrup over the fruit; toss gently to coat. Cover and chill in the refrigerator for at least 1 hour. Serve cold.

See photo on previous spread

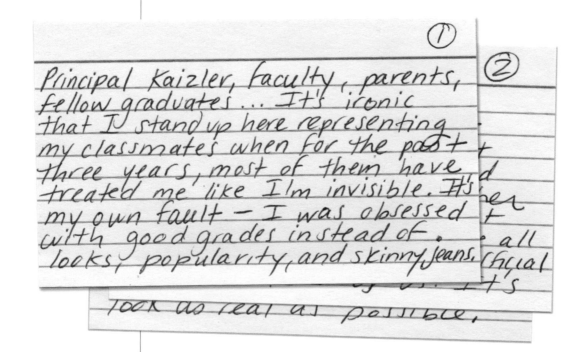

andy's | blueberry-pomegranate smoothie

Makes about 2½ cups; serves 4

2 cups frozen blueberries

1 cup 100% pomegranate juice, chilled

1 tablespoon honey

1 (6-ounce) carton fat-free vanilla yogurt

1 Put all the ingredients in a blender and process until smooth. Serve immediately.

TIP: For a tart and refreshing variation that's lower in sugar but still packs a flavor punch, use plain yogurt and omit the honey.

Season 5, Episode 6

ANDY:

Good morning, boss, junior boss. Grab a seat and check it out. Egg-white omelet, high-protein smoothies, then I thought we could put on our running shoes and go—

JAY:

I need to cut you off right there, chief. Seems my wife overstepped her bounds. Now, you seem like a nice guy . . . but I don't think you're the best fit for this house.

ANDY:

Are—are you serious?

JAY:

I'm afraid so.

ANDY:

Okay. It was the underpants, wasn't it?

manny's | french toast sticks

Serves 6

3 **large eggs**

1 **teaspoon vanilla extract**

½ **teaspoon ground cinnamon**

⅛ **teaspoon kosher salt**

1 **cup milk**

6 **slices Italian bread, halved lengthwise**

Cooking spray

¼ **cup maple syrup**

1 **cup hulled strawberries**

1 **tablespoon confectioners' sugar (optional)**

1 Preheat the oven to 250°F. Put a baking sheet in the oven.

2 Combine the eggs, vanilla, cinnamon, and salt in a medium bowl, stirring with a whisk. Add the milk; whisk until well blended. Working in batches, dip the bread strips in the milk mixture, turning gently to coat both sides.

3 Heat a large skillet over medium-high heat. Coat with cooking spray. Add 6 coated bread strips to the pan; cook for 1 to 2 minutes on each side or until lightly browned. Place on the preheated pan in the oven to keep warm. Repeat with more cooking spray and the remaining bread strips.

4 Put the syrup and strawberries in a food processor; process until smooth. Serve with the French toast sticks, sprinkling each serving with confectioners' sugar, if desired.

JAY:

Let's go, buddy. School time. Oh, and, Gloria, if you wanna get together with the girls later, I could just, you know, watch the football game or something.

MANNY:

That means he wants to watch a football game.

JAY:

I'm not talking to you. And what are you drinking coffee for, anyway?

MANNY:

It's my culture. I'm Colombian.

JAY:

Oh, yeah? What part of Colombia are those French toaster sticks from?

MANNY'S FRENCH PRESS BREW GUIDE

There are several different schools of thought when it comes to brewing coffee in a French press—more or less ground coffee, coarser or finer grind, shorter or longer brew time, and so on. Here's the basic technique Manny uses, and where he'd suggest you start your French press odyssey.

Coarsely grind good-quality coffee beans just before brewing: The coffee should be about the consistency of steel-cut oats—that is, the grains should be significantly larger than those of your average coffee ground for drip brewing.

Spoon about 70 grams (say, a scant cup) of coffee into the bottom of a 1-liter (4-cup) French press (use more or less coffee in future batches based on bean type, roast style, and your personal preference).

Bring 1 liter (4 cups) of water to a boil in a kettle and pour it over the grounds. After 15 seconds, stir to make sure that all of the grounds are soaked. Put the lid on the French press. Let brew undisturbed for 4 to 7 minutes (here, again, you'll need to do some trial and error).

Very, very slowly, press the plunger all the way down. Pour the coffee into cups and enjoy.

manny's coffee evolution

Manny Delgado is passionate about many things—fine suits, pretty ladies, romantic poetry—but a good cup of joe may be his biggest weakness. Follow his journey from caffeine junkie to coffee connoisseur below, and learn how to brew from the best.

"I honestly can't see myself going back to drip."

SEASON 1 • EP 5 • COAL DIGGER

Jay questions why Manny drinks coffee.

JAY:
What are you drinking coffee for, anyway?

MANNY:
It's my culture. I'm Colombian.

SEASON 2 • EP 3 • EARTHQUAKE

Manny starts drinking his coffee light and sweet.

JAY:
You know, it might be easier just to pour the espresso right in the sugar.

MANNY, CHUCKLING:
Every morning.

SEASON 2 • EP 5 • UNPLUGGED

**Jay points out that
Manny's habit is unusual.**

JAY:
Don't most kids drink soda?

MANNY:
Who knows what they do?

SEASON 2 • EP 20 • SOMEONE TO
WATCH OVER LILY

**Manny starts using a
coffee press and no longer
settles for the drip.**

MANNY:
Say yes. It's French press. I was
doubtful too, but I honestly can't
see myself going back to drip.

SEASON 4 • EP 16 • BAD HAIR DAY

**Manny switches to black after
losing a third singing audition.**

MANNY:
Just coffee for me today.
Black, like I feel on the inside.

MANNY:

Whoa, whoa, whoa—
what is this? Where's my
soft-boiled egg?

GLORIA:

I scrambled it. It's good for
you to try new things.

MANNY:

I don't wanna try new
things. You can't just
spring this on me.

GLORIA:

I have got bad news,
Manny. This is not the
biggest curveball that life
is going to throw at you.

manny's | soft-boiled eggs

Serves 4

4 large eggs
Kosher salt and freshly ground
   black pepper

1 Put the eggs in a medium saucepan. Add water to cover the eggs by 1 inch.
   Put the lid on the pan and bring to a boil over high heat. Remove from the
   heat; leave eggs, covered, in the hot water for 1 to 4 minutes, depending on
   desired degree of doneness.

2 Remove the eggs from the pan with a slotted spoon; place in a bowl of ice
   water until cool enough to handle. Break the shell at the widest point with
   a knife. Scoop the egg out of each shell and serve immediately, with salt
   and pepper.

claire's | scrambled eggs

Serves 4 to 6

9 eggs, beaten

½ cup unsalted butter or margarine, melted

1 tablespoon whipping cream

1 Combine the eggs and butter in a medium mixing bowl, stirring well. Add the cream and mix well. Pour the egg mixture into a medium saucepan; cook over medium heat, stirring often, until the eggs are firm but still moist. Spoon onto a warm serving platter and serve immediately.

TIP: For an extra-light and fluffy scramble, use milk instead of cream and increase the quantity to ¼ cup.

TIP: For a more substantial breakfast, lightly sauté some vegetables in the butter in the saucepan over medium-low heat until just tender, then add the beaten eggs and continue to cook until firm. Try any combination of diced sweet onion, diced red or green bell peppers (or minced hot peppers), sweet corn kernels, frozen peas (no need to defrost), and finely chopped broccoli or cauliflower.

Season 5, Episode 6

ALEX, OFFSCREEN:
You're ruining my life!

PHIL:
These eggs are delicious.

CLAIRE:
Mmm.

HALEY, OFFSCREEN:
What life?! Get out of my room!

CLAIRE:
I put milk in them.

PHIL:
Oh.

"Kids these days get trophies just for showing up. What's that gonna lead to? A bunch of thirty-year-olds living at home."

—CLAIRE

MITCHELL:

People can surprise you. You get used to thinking of them one way, stuck in their roles. They are what they are. And then they do something that shows you there's all this depth and dimension that you never knew existed.

CAM:

Are you talking about Rob Lowe?

MITCHELL:

I'm just saying he's a very versatile actor. I think his good looks have actually held him back.

CAM:

Yeah. I can relate to that.

mitchell's | vegetable-gruyère quiche

Serves 4

1 cup julienned leeks	1 large egg white
2 cups julienned zucchini	2 tablespoons milk
2 cups julienned yellow squash	1 teaspoon dried Italian seasoning
1 cup julienned red bell pepper	½ teaspoon kosher salt
1⅓ cups all-purpose flour	¼ teaspoon freshly ground black pepper
¼ cup unsalted butter or margarine	¼ cup (1 ounce) finely grated Gruyère cheese
2 large eggs	

1 Preheat the oven to 450°F.

2 Bring 2 inches of water to a boil in a pot. Add the leeks; cover and simmer for 5 minutes. Add the zucchini, squash, and bell pepper; simmer for 5 minutes. Drain well and pat dry.

3 Put the flour in a bowl; cut in the butter with a pastry blender until the mixture resembles coarse meal. Sprinkle 2 to 3 tablespoons cold water evenly over the surface of the mixture; stir with a fork until the flour is moistened. Shape into a ball. Place between two sheets of heavy-duty plastic wrap and gently press into a 4-inch circle. Chill for 20 minutes. Roll into a 12-inch circle. Freeze for 5 minutes. Unwrap and fit the pastry into a 9-inch pie plate. Fold the edges of the pastry under and flute; seal to the edge of the quiche dish. Bake the pastry for 5 minutes. Spoon the vegetable mixture into the pastry. Let stand for 5 minutes.

4 Combine the whole eggs, egg white, milk, Italian seasoning, salt, and pepper; stir well with a wire whisk. Pour over the vegetable mixture. Bake for 30 minutes; sprinkle with the cheese. Bake for 5 additional minutes or until the cheese melts. Let stand for 5 minutes before serving.

NOTE: You can substitute a frozen pie shell if you want to save a little time (preferably one with no sugar added).

mitchell's | breakfast burritos

Serves 8

1 (15-ounce) can black beans, drained

2 teaspoons fresh lime juice

Cooking spray

6 large eggs, lightly beaten

8 (8-inch) flour tortillas

1 cup fresh salsa

2 ounces crumbled cotija or feta cheese (about ½ cup)

1 Put the beans and lime juice in a small bowl; mash with the back of a spoon until almost smooth.

2 Heat a large skillet over medium-high heat. Coat the pan with cooking spray. Add the eggs to the pan and cook, without stirring, until they set on the bottom. Draw a spatula across the eggs to form curds. Continue cooking, stirring occasionally, until the eggs are thickened but still moist. Remove from the pan immediately.

3 Wipe out the skillet and place it over medium heat. Coat the pan with cooking spray. Add 1 tortilla to the pan. Heat for 20 seconds on each side or just until soft. Remove from the pan and cover to keep warm. Repeat with the remaining tortillas.

4 Spoon 2 tablespoons of the bean mixture, 2½ tablespoons of the eggs, 2 tablespoons of the salsa, and 1 tablespoon cheese down the center of each tortilla. Roll up, folding in the ends to completely enclose the filling. Coat the skillet with cooking spray again. Put the burritos in the pan and cook over medium heat, turning occasionally, for 4 minutes or until lightly browned. Serve hot, or wrap in waxed paper to take with you.

Season 1, Episode 5

CAM:

You know what? You need to loosen up and have fun.

MITCHELL:

I am loose. I'm fun. Remember, uh, breakfast for dinner last week. That was my idea.

cam's | grandmother's housekeeper delilah's biscuits *and* gravy

Serves 6

- 2 cups plus 2½ tablespoons all-purpose flour, plus more for the work surface
- 3¼ teaspoons baking powder
- ½ teaspoon baking soda
- ¾ teaspoon kosher salt
- ¼ cup vegetable shortening
- 1 cup buttermilk

- Cooking spray
- 4 ounces pork breakfast sausage
- 1 teaspoon unsalted butter
- 1 cup chopped onion
- 2¼ cups milk
- 2 teaspoons minced fresh sage
- 1 teaspoon freshly ground black pepper

1 Preheat the oven to 450°F.

2 Combine 2 cups of the flour, the baking powder, baking soda, and ½ teaspoon of the salt in a bowl; cut in the shortening with a pastry blender or two knives until the mixture resembles coarse meal. Add the buttermilk; stir just until moist.

3 Turn the dough out onto a heavily floured surface; knead lightly five times. Roll the dough to ½-inch thickness; cut with a 3¼-inch biscuit cutter. Put the biscuits on a baking sheet coated with cooking spray. Bake for 10 minutes or until golden.

4 Cook the sausage in a large nonstick skillet over medium-high heat for 10 minutes or until browned; stir to crumble. Remove from the pan and drain on paper towels. Add the butter to the drippings in the pan; cook until the butter melts. Add the onion; cook for 12 minutes, stirring frequently. Stir in the sausage, 2 cups of the milk, the sage, the remaining ¼ teaspoon salt, and the pepper.

5 Combine the remaining 2½ tablespoons flour and the remaining ¼ cup milk, stirring with a whisk until well blended to form a slurry. Stir the slurry into the sausage mixture. Cook, stirring constantly, for 3 minutes or until the gravy is thick and bubbly. Split the biscuits in half. Spoon the gravy evenly over the biscuit halves and serve immediately.

Season 3, Episode 14

JAY:

Biscuits and gravy?

CAM:

Yep. My grandma Bitsy's secret recipe, given to her by her housekeeper, Delilah, who raised her and was her best friend. Kind of like *The Help*, except Delilah was white, and was actually herself quite the racist. Eat up.

cam's | grilled farmhouse breakfast

Serves 4

8 large eggs	¼ teaspoon kosher salt
Unsalted butter	¼ teaspoon freshly ground black pepper
4 (1-inch-thick) slices crusty bread	
	1 garlic clove, cut in half; or jam
8 thick slices bacon	

1 Prepare a grill for direct cooking over medium heat (350° to 450°F).

2 Crack all the eggs gently into a large bowl. Butter the bread slices on both sides.

3 Brush the cooking grates clean. Arrange the bacon in a single layer in a 12-inch cast-iron skillet. Grill over direct medium heat, with the grill lid closed as much as possible, until crisp, 15 to 20 minutes, turning and rearranging the bacon as it cooks and shrinks. Drain the bacon on paper towels and then wrap in foil and keep warm on the grill's warming rack or in a low oven.

4 Use a large serving spoon to scoop out about half of the bacon grease from the skillet, leaving a ⅛-inch layer on the bottom. Gently pour all the eggs into the skillet at once and season with the salt and pepper. Place the bread directly on the grill and cook both the eggs and the bread over direct medium heat, with the lid closed as much as possible, until the eggs begin to cloud over on top (the yolks will be partially runny) and the bread is toasted. The eggs will take 4 to 6 minutes, and the toast will take 3 to 4 minutes. Turn the bread once during grilling. Transfer the toast to the warming rack or oven with the bacon.

5 Using a serving spoon or spatula, cut the eggs apart and scoop them out of the skillet one at a time. If savory toast is desired, rub each side with the cut side of the garlic clove while the toast is still warm. If sweet toast is preferred, spread it with jam. Serve the eggs and toast immediately with the bacon.

Season 5, Episode 8

CAM:

Daddy went to town. He's gonna be there till supper, so I'm helping Mama slop the pigs. You want to— you want to pitch in?

MITCHELL:

I don't know. I just ate that bacon, so . . . how's that gonna look?

SNACKS, HORS D'OEUVRES, *and* PARTY FOODS

alex's | brain food energy bars

Makes 16 (3-by-1½-inch) bars

2 cups quinoa flakes

1 cup sliced almonds

½ cup roasted, salted sunflower seeds

½ cup wheat germ

2 tablespoons chia seeds

2 tablespoons protein powder

¼ cup goji berries

½ cup golden raisins

½ cup dried cherries

4 tablespoons unsalted butter, plus more for the baking sheet

½ cup plus 2 tablespoons light brown sugar

½ cup plus 2 tablespoons agave syrup

1½ teaspoons vanilla extract

Scant ½ teaspoon kosher salt

1 Preheat the oven to 350°F.

2 On a rimmed baking sheet, combine the quinoa flakes and almonds and toast until golden and fragrant, about 10 minutes. Transfer to a large bowl and stir in the sunflower seeds, wheat germ, chia seeds, protein powder, goji berries, raisins, and dried cherries. Line the baking sheet with buttered parchment paper.

3 In a medium saucepan, combine the 4 tablespoons butter with the brown sugar and agave and bring to a boil. Cook over medium heat, stirring, until the sugar is just dissolved, about 2 minutes. Add the vanilla and salt. Pour the mixture into the bowl and stir until completely combined. Scrape the mixture onto the parchment and form it into a 6-inch-by-12-inch rectangle, pressing it lightly to compact. Use something with a straight edge to evenly press the sides. Bake in the center of the oven for 10 minutes, until very lightly browned. Let cool slightly, then refrigerate until firm, about 20 minutes.

4 Invert the bar onto a cutting board and peel off the paper. Cut the bar into four 3-inch strips, then cut each strip into four 1½-inch bars. Serve right away, or wrap in plastic. The wrapped bars can be stored at room temperature for up to 1 week or refrigerated for up to 2 weeks.

Season 5, Episode 20

ALEX, INTO IPHONE:
Sometimes, one must travel halfway across the globe to get the clearest view of home.

HALEY:
This was my whole flight.

MITCHELL:
What's she talking about?

ALEX:
My college-application essay. They want students who are worldly.

MITCHELL:
Oh, why don't you write about our trip to Hawaii when you drank straight from a coconut?

ALEX:
I feel like Harvard's gonna get a lot of those, so . . .

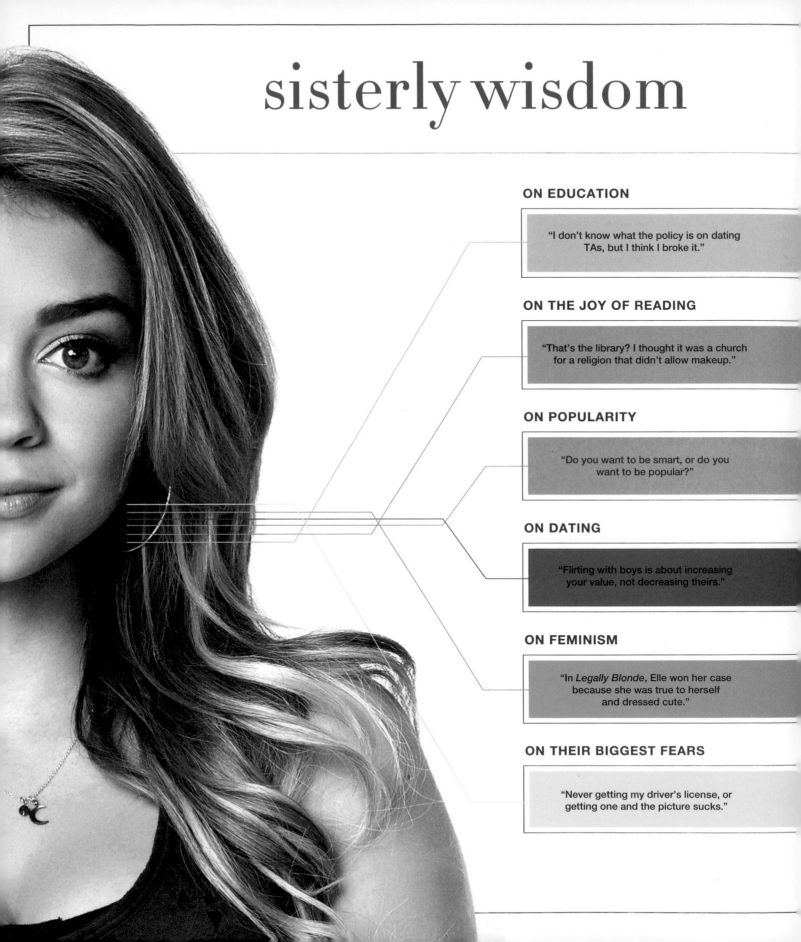

sisterly wisdom

ON EDUCATION

"I don't know what the policy is on dating TAs, but I think I broke it."

ON THE JOY OF READING

"That's the library? I thought it was a church for a religion that didn't allow makeup."

ON POPULARITY

"Do you want to be smart, or do you want to be popular?"

ON DATING

"Flirting with boys is about increasing your value, not decreasing theirs."

ON FEMINISM

"In *Legally Blonde*, Elle won her case because she was true to herself and dressed cute."

ON THEIR BIGGEST FEARS

"Never getting my driver's license, or getting one and the picture sucks."

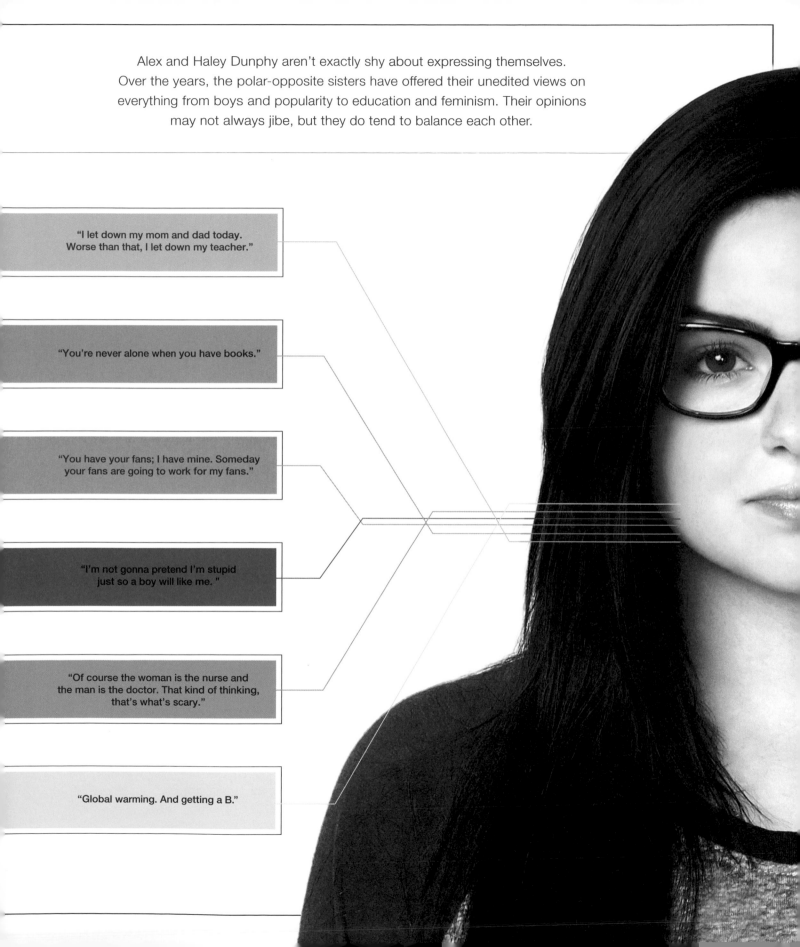

Alex and Haley Dunphy aren't exactly shy about expressing themselves. Over the years, the polar-opposite sisters have offered their unedited views on everything from boys and popularity to education and feminism. Their opinions may not always jibe, but they do tend to balance each other.

"I let down my mom and dad today. Worse than that, I let down my teacher."

"You're never alone when you have books."

"You have your fans; I have mine. Someday your fans are going to work for my fans."

"I'm not gonna pretend I'm stupid just so a boy will like me."

"Of course the woman is the nurse and the man is the doctor. That kind of thinking, that's what's scary."

"Global warming. And getting a B."

joe's | fruit-yogurt pops

1 cup strawberries, hulled
¾ cup blueberries
¾ cup raspberries
1 small ripe banana

2 tablespoons fresh lemon juice
2 cups vanilla yogurt
¼ cup sugar

1 Put the strawberries, blueberries, raspberries, banana, and lemon juice in a blender; process until smooth. Press the mixture through a sieve over a bowl; discard the solids. Return the fruit mixture to the blender. Add the yogurt and sugar; process until smooth.

2 Pour the yogurt mixture into 2½-ounce Popsicle molds according to the manufacturer's instructions. Freeze for 3 hours.

NOTE: No ice-pop molds on hand? Pour the mixture into small paper cups, cover with foil, and stick Popsicle sticks through the foil while they freeze.

KIDS CAN HELP! Young chefs can help by washing the strawberries and adding the fruit to the blender. Older chefs can help by hulling the strawberries with adult supervision and pressing the mixture through the sieve.

Season 5, Episode 11

JOE, TO ANDY:
Dada.

ANDY:
No, no, no, little man. That's your dada right there with the drinky.

JAY:
Overexplaining.

ANDY:
Don't feel bad. He's just making sounds. He may not even know what the "D" word means.

JAY:
I'm fine. I've watched him pee into his own face and smile.

JAY:

Welcome to Jay's Night. Names, please. Want to make sure you're on the list. Kidding! Just excited. Appetizers on the bar, Scrabble on the coffee table, and our feature presentation, *The Great Escape*. Speaking of which, Haley . . .

HALEY:

Don't worry, Grandpa. I'm not leaving. I have no plans for the night.

ALEX:

Me, either.

HALEY:

But when I say it, it's news.

ALEX:

When you say any complete sentence, it's news.

jay's | movie night cinnamon-sugar popcorn

Makes 10 cups

10 cups popcorn (popped without salt or fat)

2 tablespoons light brown sugar

1 teaspoon ground cinnamon

⅛ teaspoon kosher salt

2 tablespoons unsalted butter, melted

Cooking spray

1 Put the popcorn in a large bowl. Combine the brown sugar, cinnamon, and salt in a small bowl. Drizzle the popcorn with the butter; toss to coat. Coat the popcorn generously with cooking spray. Sprinkle with the sugar mixture; toss well and serve immediately.

KIDS CAN HELP!

While the popcorn pops, kids can measure the cinnamon-sugar mixture and then toss it with the popcorn and butter.

mitchell's | so-cal tomatillo-avocado dip

Makes about 1¼ cups

8 **tomatillos**	1 **Hass avocado**
2 **garlic cloves**	1 **tablespoon fresh lime juice**
1 **jalapeño pepper, halved and seeded**	¼ **cup tightly packed fresh cilantro**
	½ **teaspoon kosher salt**

1 Preheat the broiler.

2 Discard the husks and stems from the tomatillos; wash thoroughly. Place the tomatillos on a foil-lined baking sheet and broil 3 inches from the heat source for 6 to 8 minutes or until the tomatillos look blistered, turning once. Let cool.

3 Process the garlic in a food processor until minced. Add the jalapeño; process until minced, stopping once to scrape down the sides.

4 Cut the avocado in half and remove the seed; cut the avocado into quarters and peel them. Add the cooled tomatillos, avocado, lime juice, cilantro, and salt to the jalapeño mixture. Process for 15 seconds or until the tomatillos are pureed. Cover and chill in the refrigerator for 1 hour.

TIP: Serve with a few batches of Baked Wonton Crisps (see page 52) for a multi-culti party snack, or toast pita triangles on a baking sheet. Or, if you need a plan C, just open a bag of tortilla chips and dig in.

Season 4, Episode 17

MITCHELL:
Oh! Our game night's on Saturday. They're epic.

CAM:
Huge. Mm-hmm.

MITCHELL:
Yeah. Do you play Cranium?

SAL:
Well, if I'm playing board games on Saturday night, you can shoot me in my cranium, but I love you!

Season 4, Episode 21

CAM:

Ooh, okay, we cannot be the parents of a six-year-old who gets $100 from the tooth fairy.

MITCHELL:

It's bad enough we're the parents of a six-year-old with a clutch.

CAM:

You know, that bag transitions from day to night seamlessly, and I no longer have to carry crayons in my front pocket.

MITCHELL:

Can't have this argument again!

cam's | baked wonton crisps

Makes 12 crisps

1½ teaspoons sesame or vegetable oil

12 wonton wrappers

1½ teaspoons sesame seeds

¼ teaspoon kosher salt

1 Preheat the oven to 400°F.

2 Combine the sesame oil with 1½ teaspoons water; brush the mixture evenly over the wonton wrappers on a baking sheet. Sprinkle the sesame seeds and salt evenly over the wonton wrappers. Bake for 5 minutes or until lightly browned and crisp. Serve warm or at room temperature.

NOTE: Different spice combinations yield dramatically different results. Try cinnamon sugar, Chinese five-spice, or a Cajun spice blend.

TIP: Serve solo or with your husband's favorite dip (see page 51).

cam's | roasted pepper *and* beef crostini

Makes 48 small bites

1 (7-ounce) bottle roasted red bell peppers, drained and chopped (about ⅔ cup)

½ cup finely chopped fresh basil

1 tablespoon extra-virgin olive oil

¼ teaspoon kosher salt

¼ teaspoon freshly ground black pepper

48 (¼-inch-thick) slices diagonally cut French baguette

Olive oil–flavored cooking spray

1 (6½-ounce) container light garlic-and-herb spreadable cheese (such as Alouette Light)

8 ounces shaved deli roast beef

1 Preheat the broiler.

2 Combine the bell peppers, basil, oil, salt, and black pepper in a bowl; stir well.

3 Coat both sides of the bread slices with cooking spray. Place half of the bread slices in a single layer on a large baking sheet. Broil for 1½ minutes on each side or until lightly toasted. Repeat with the remaining bread.

4 Spread 1 teaspoon of the cheese over one side of each slice of toast. Divide the beef evenly among the toasts; top each with 1 teaspoon of the bell pepper mixture. Serve immediately.

NOTE: Use the best deli roast beef you can find, and, if you like, substitute soft goat cheese or Brie for the cheese spread.

Season 2, Episode 8

CAM:
I appreciate the gesture, and I'm not proud of how I'm feeling right now, but the fact is, you cheated on me.

MITCHELL:
In what way did I—

CAM:
You cheated on me with choreography, and that is the worst kind.

MITCHELL:
Well, it really isn't.

CAM:
You danced without me, Mitchell!

Season 1, Episode 12

CLAIRE:

Okay, I checked the rest of the computers in the house. I didn't find any more porn.

PHIL:

That was hardly porn. It was a topless woman on a tractor. You know what they call that in Europe? A cereal commercial.

claire's | honey-peppered goat cheese *with* fig balsamic drizzle

Serves 6 to 8

1 (11-ounce) package or 4 (3-ounce) logs fresh goat cheese

⅓ cup extra-virgin olive oil

¼ cup honey

½ teaspoon freshly ground black pepper

1 teaspoon fresh thyme leaves, plus more for garnish

Fig balsamic vinegar (see Note) or balsamic vinegar

Lavash or other specialty cracker bread

1 Using a sharp knife, carefully cut the goat cheese into ½-inch-thick slices. Place the cheese in an 11-by-7-inch dish or other serving platter. Drizzle with the oil. Combine the honey and pepper; drizzle over the cheese. Sprinkle with the thyme leaves. Cover and chill in the refrigerator for up to 2 days.

2 Remove the cheese from refrigerator 1 hour before serving. Just before serving, drizzle a little vinegar over the cheese. Garnish, if desired, with more thyme. Serve with lavash.

NOTE: You can find fig balsamic vinegar at Williams-Sonoma and other specialty stores.

TIP: Alternatively, you can serve rounds of drizzled goat cheese on individual plates at the start or end of a meal.

Search for ideas  Claire

Halloween Ideas

Holiday Planning

Claire Dunphy Invite

123
Pins

62
Followers

Move Pins | Edit Board | •••

Add a Pin

Bloody Zombie Chick

Pinned from
sicker-than-you

Sexy Creepy Stud — PHIL!!!

Pinned from
Uploaded by user

Gory Zombie Bride — to pair with creepy stud

Pinned from
zombiegirl129

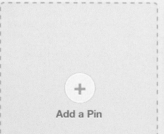

Doctor-Clown Zombie — Luke?

Pinned from
deadlydawn

Scary Skull

Pinned from
horrorluvr

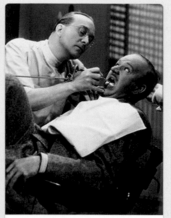

Maniacal Dentist

Pinned from
Pete Robinson

Spooky Haunted House

Pinned from
creepymarc

**Halloween Cocktails
(+Swampwater Punch!)**

Pinned from
Marge Stevenson

Bloody Mess!

Pinned from
Uploaded by user

Medical Terror!

Pinned from
devildeepinside

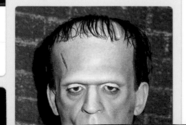

claire's | spooky pumpkin cheese ball *with* crudités

Makes 1 pumpkin-shaped cheese ball (4 cups)

2 **(8-ounce) packages shredded extra-sharp Cheddar cheese**

1 **(8-ounce) package cream cheese, softened**

1 **(8-ounce) container chive-and-onion cream cheese**

2 **teaspoons paprika, plus more for decoration**

½ **teaspoon ground red pepper**

1 **broccoli stalk**

Apple wedges, crackers, or carrot and celery sticks

1 Combine the Cheddar cheese, cream cheeses, the 2 teaspoons paprika, and the red pepper in a large bowl. Beat at medium speed with an electric mixer until blended. Cover with plastic wrap and chill in the refrigerator for at least 1 hour.

2 Shape the cheese mixture into a ball and place on a flat serving plate. Using the handle of a wooden spoon, make vertical grooves in the ball to resemble a pumpkin, and dust the grooves with a little more paprika. Cover the cheese ball with plastic wrap and refrigerate for up to 5 days. Cut florets from the broccoli; save them to eat later. Trim small leaves from the broccoli stalk. Cut the stalk to look like a pumpkin stem; press into top of the cheese ball along with small leaves from the broccoli. Serve with apple wedges, crackers, and/or vegetables.

Season 4, Episode 5

CLAIRE:
What do you mean, I'm not even scary? I literally almost scared the life out of a man.

PHIL:
You literally scared a little saliva and a little urine out of him. That happens to me every time I see a monkey wearing people clothes.

CLAIRE:
I was plenty scary. I used professional-grade makeup.

PHIL:
That's the point, Claire. It was overkill. You're the kind of person who can be twice as scary without wearing any makeup.

Season 6, Episode 6

PHIL:
Claire loves blood and guts and gore, but who says Halloween has to be scary?

CLAIRE:
Everybody but you.

PHIL:
This is killing her.

CLAIRE:
At least something's dying.

phil's | monster eyes

Makes about 54 sausage balls

3 cups all-purpose baking mix

1 pound ground mild or hot pork sausage

1 (10-ounce) block extra-sharp Cheddar cheese, shredded

54 small pimiento-stuffed olives

1 Preheat the oven to 400°F.

2 Combine the baking mix, sausage, and cheese in a large bowl. Stir with a wooden spoon until blended. Shape the sausage mixture into 1-inch balls and place them on lightly greased baking sheets. Press 1 olive deeply into each ball. Reroll using the palms of your hands if you need to reshape. Bake for 22 minutes or until lightly browned. Serve hot or warm.

3 You can freeze Monster Eyes in an airtight container for up to 1 month. To reheat, place the frozen balls on an ungreased baking sheet and bake at 350°F for 10 minutes or until heated through.

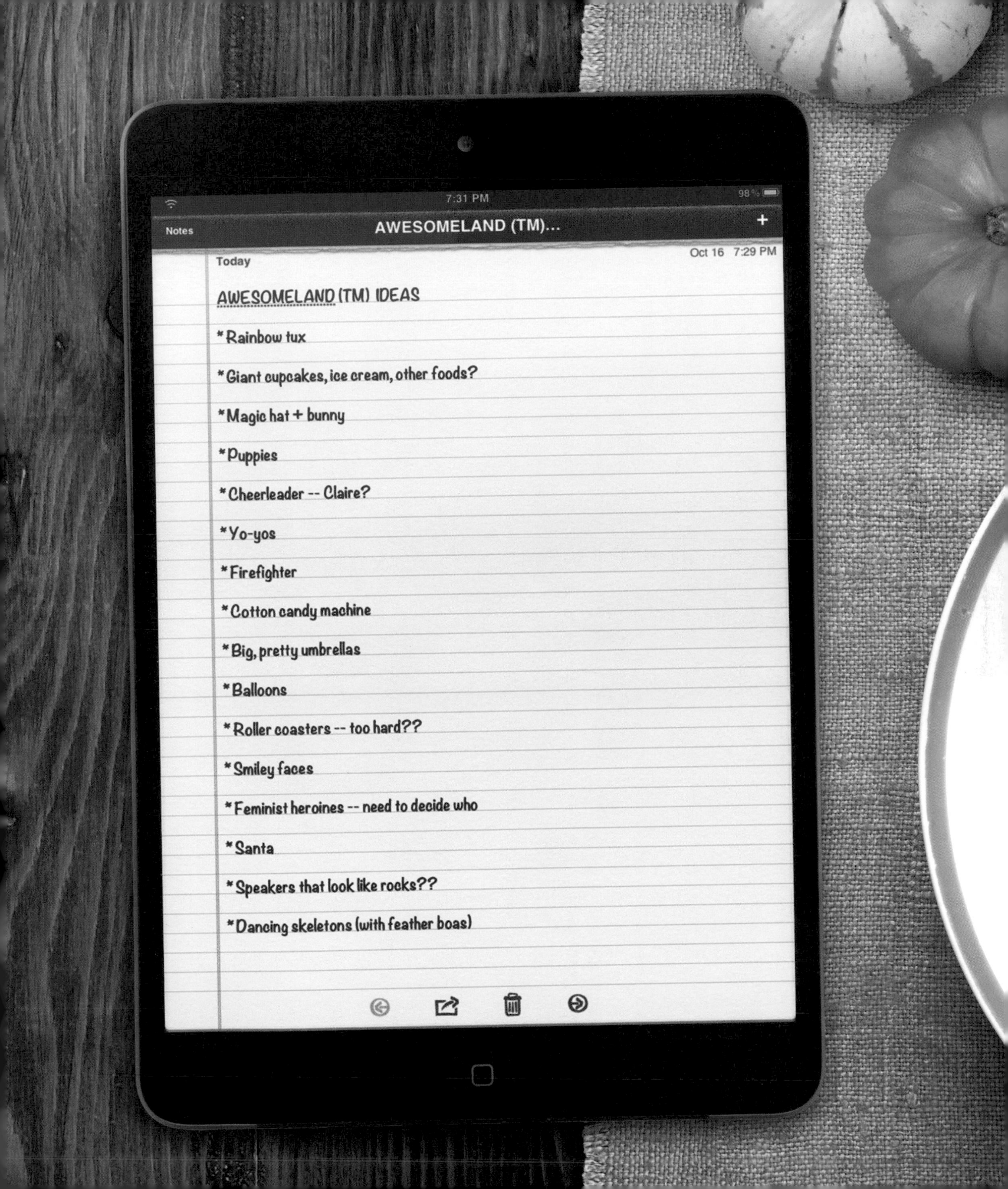
7:31 PM
98 %
Notes
AWESOMELAND (TM)...
+
Today
Oct 16 7:29 PM
AWESOMELAND (TM) IDEAS
* Rainbow tux
* Giant cupcakes, ice cream, other foods?
* Magic hat + bunny
* Puppies
* Cheerleader -- Claire?
* Yo-yos
* Firefighter
* Cotton candy machine
* Big, pretty umbrellas
* Balloons
* Roller coasters -- too hard??
* Smiley faces
* Feminist heroines -- need to decide who
* Santa
* Speakers that look like rocks??
* Dancing skeletons (with feather boas)

gloria's | empanadas

Makes 32 empanadas; serves 8 to 10

FOR THE FILLING:

Kosher salt

1 large russet potato (8 ounces), peeled and cut into ½-inch pieces

1 tablespoon vegetable oil

1 small white onion, minced (1 cup)

2 garlic cloves, minced

1 pound ground beef

1½ tablespoons ground cumin

1 (8-ounce) can tomato sauce

½ cup sliced green pimento-stuffed olives

2 tablespoons drained, rinsed capers

Freshly ground black pepper

FOR THE DOUGH:

3 to 3½ cups hot water

1 tablespoon lard or unsalted butter

1 scant teaspoon sugar

1 scant teaspoon kosher salt

3 cups masa for arepas (precooked instant cornmeal, such as masarepa, P.A.N., or harina de maiz)

Vegetable oil for frying

FOR THE SALSA:

1 large ripe tomato, chopped

1 scallion, thinly sliced

2 tablespoons chopped fresh cilantro

1½ teaspoons aji amarillo or other hot sauce to taste

Kosher salt

Season 2, Episode 1

GLORIA:
Manny, why don't you give your friend Kelly an empanada?

KELLY:
Oh, no thank you. I try to stay away from trans fats.

GLORIA:
I'm sure one won't make a difference. They're Manny's favorite.

MANNY:
I think I'm going to stop eating trans fats, too.

1 Make the filling: Bring a small pot of salted water to a boil. Add the potato and cook until tender, about 8 minutes. Drain and pat dry.

2 In a deep skillet, heat the oil. Cook the onion and garlic over medium heat, stirring occasionally, until softened, 6 to 7 minutes. Add the beef and cumin and cook, stirring occasionally, until no longer pink, 6 to 7 minutes. Add the potatoes and cook until lightly browned, about 2 minutes. Mash coarsely. Add the tomato sauce, olives, and capers and simmer over low heat until very thick and the sauce is completely reduced, about 5 minutes. Season with salt and pepper and let cool.

3 Make the dough: In a large bowl, combine 3 cups of the hot water with the lard, sugar, and salt. Add the masa and stir until evenly combined. Turn

continued on next page

the dough out onto a work surface and knead briefly until smooth. Wrap in plastic and let sit for 15 minutes.

4 Divide the dough into 32 balls and keep them covered with plastic. Line a large baking sheet with waxed paper. Working with one or two balls at a time and using the palms of your hands or a tortilla press, flatten them into 4-inch rounds. Spoon a slightly rounded tablespoon of the filling into the center. Fold into a half-moon and pinch the edges, pressing to seal. Transfer the finished empanadas to a waxed paper–lined tray and keep covered with plastic wrap to prevent the dough from drying out and cracking.

5 Fill a large pot with 2 inches of oil and heat it to 350°F. Working in batches, fry the empanadas over medium heat, maintaining 350°F, until golden and crisp, about 6 minutes. Drain on paper towels.

6 Make the salsa: In a mini chopper, combine the tomato, scallion, and cilantro and pulse until finely chopped. Add the hot sauce and season with salt. Serve with the empanadas.

"What kind of man writes poetry on the computer?"

—MANNY

manny's | charcuterie plate

MEATS:

Prosciutto

Bresaola

Dry-cured sausage

Jamón serrano

Soppressata

Pâté (de campagne or mousse truffée)

CHEESES:

Brie, Camembert, or Taleggio

Aged Cheddar or goat Gouda

Manchego or fresh pecorino

Gorgonzola or Stilton

Fresh goat cheese

ACCOMPANIMENTS:

Dried fruit (apricots, cherries, figs)

Membrillo (quince paste or other paste)

Grapes

Persimmons

Pears

Nuts (walnuts, almonds, Marcona almonds, hazelnuts)

Olives

Small toasts, sliced nut bread, or crackers

CONDIMENTS:

Mustard (such as Homemade Grainy Mustard; recipe follows)

Chutney (such as Apricot-Fig Chutney; recipe follows)

NOTE: To serve twelve people, choose five cheeses (6 ounces each), four meats (6 ounces each), two fruits (8–12 ounces total), one or two condiments (4 ounces total), olives (8 ounces), nuts (4 ounces), and either a baguette or a box or two of crackers. For two people, the plate certainly doesn't have to be an elaborate, farm-to-table, restaurant-style affair. One or two cheeses, a meat or two, some nuts, and a dollop of a special condiment of some sort will do.

continued on next page

Season 3, Episode 24

JAY:

What's that?

MANNY:

It's charcuterie. You got your prosciutto, your pancetta, your salami.

JAY:

That's charcuterie? I've been avoiding that on menus for years. They're killing themselves with that name.

homemade grainy mustard

Makes 1 cup

⅔ cup dry white wine

3 tablespoons yellow mustard seeds (see Note)

3 tablespoons brown mustard seeds

1 tablespoon minced shallot

½ teaspoon kosher salt

⅛ teaspoon ground turmeric

1 teaspoon prepared horseradish

1 Combine the wine, mustard seeds, shallot, salt, and turmeric in a glass, stainless-steel, or other nonreactive bowl. Cover and refrigerate for 2 days.

2 Put the mustard mixture and horseradish in a blender; process until coarsely ground. Transfer to a glass jar. Cover and store in the refrigerator for up to 1 month.

NOTE: Look for mustard seeds in Indian grocery stores, where they'll be fresh and reasonably priced.

apricot-fig chutney

Makes 2½ cups

3 cups apricots, peeled, pitted, and quartered

½ cup dried figs, quartered

½ cup white wine

⅓ cup sugar

¼ cup golden raisins

1½ teaspoons chopped fresh thyme

1 tablespoon honey

1 tablespoon fresh lemon juice

1 teaspoon mustard seeds

½ teaspoon cumin seeds

½ teaspoon ground ginger

¼ teaspoon kosher salt

Dash of ground red pepper

½ jalapeño pepper, finely chopped

½ shallot, sliced

2 tablespoons chopped fresh cilantro

1 Combine all the ingredients except the cilantro in a large Dutch oven over medium heat and bring to a simmer. Cook for 15 minutes. If you're storing the chutney for later use, let cool, then transfer to an airtight container and keep in the refrigerator for up to 3 months. Stir in the cilantro just before serving at room temperature.

jay's | crab cakes *with* jalapeño-lime tartar sauce

Season 2, Episode 18

JAY:
Buddy, don't close yourself off from new things. Ever tell you the story about me and crab cakes? Thought I didn't like 'em. Tried them. Love them.

MANNY:
Wow. Are the movie rights available for that one?

Serves 6

1 sleeve saltine crackers (about 37 crackers)

¼ cup mayonnaise

¼ cup sour cream

1 large egg

⅓ cup minced fresh chives

2 (6-ounce) cans lump crabmeat, drained

1 medium tomato, seeded and chopped

1 tablespoon canola oil

Jalapeño-Lime Tartar Sauce (recipe follows)

1 Put the crackers in a food processor; process until finely ground.

2 Combine the mayonnaise, sour cream, and egg in a large bowl; stir with a whisk. Stir in 1 cup of the cracker crumbs and the chives. Gently fold in the crabmeat and tomato. Form the mixture into 6 (1-inch-thick) patties. Dredge the crab cakes in the remaining cracker crumbs. Chill in the refrigerator for 30 minutes.

3 Heat the oil in a large nonstick skillet over medium-high heat. Add the crab cakes and cook for 4 to 5 minutes on each side or until browned. Serve immediately with the tartar sauce.

NOTE: Be sure to chill the shaped crab cakes in the fridge before you pan-fry them: They'll hold their shape much better.

jalapeño-lime tartar sauce

Makes about ¾ cup

⅓ cup mayonnaise

⅓ cup sour cream

2 tablespoons dill pickle relish

1 teaspoon grated lime zest

1 jalapeño pepper, seeded and minced

⅛ teaspoon kosher salt

1 Combine all the ingredients in a small bowl; cover and chill in the refrigerator until ready to serve.

Season 3, Episode 3

SERVER:

Goat cheese risotto ball?

CAM:

No, thank you.

SERVER:

**Are you sure? They're
so good.**

CAM:

Walk away.

cam's | healthy tabbouleh-style rice cucumber rounds

Makes 32

- 1 **cup cooked brown rice**
- 6 **tablespoons finely grated
  Asiago cheese**
- ¼ **cup finely chopped fresh
  flat-leaf parsley**
- ¼ **cup finely chopped roasted
  red bell peppers**
- 1 **tablespoon chopped fresh
  oregano**
- 3 **tablespoons drained capers**

- 2 **teaspoons grated lemon zest**
- 1 **tablespoon fresh lemon juice**
- 2 **tablespoons extra-virgin olive oil**
- ¼ **teaspoon salt**
- ⅛ **teaspoon crushed red pepper**
- 2 **garlic cloves, minced**
- 32 **(¼-inch-thick) English cucumber
  slices (about 1 cucumber)**

1 Combine all the ingredients except the cucumber; toss gently. Spoon 1 rounded
tablespoon rice mixture onto each cucumber slice.

Mr. Pepper Saltyman
374 Sycamore Lane
Calabasas, CA 91302

Mr. Cameron & Mit
276 Cresthill Aven
Oak Park, CA 9137

pepper's | citrus, fennel, *and* rosemary olives

Makes about 5 cups

22 ounces (about 4 cups) assorted olives (such as Niçoise, Arbequina, Kalamata, and picholine)

2 cups extra-virgin olive oil

1 cup finely chopped fennel bulb

1 tablespoon chopped fresh flat-leaf parsley

1½ teaspoons chopped fresh rosemary

1 teaspoon grated lemon zest

¾ teaspoon crushed red pepper

3 garlic cloves, minced

1 Combine all the ingredients in a large bowl; stir well. Cover and refrigerate for at least 48 hours and up to 1 month. Serve at room temperature.

PEPPER SALTZMAN
CORDIALLY INVITES YOU TO:

SEDER-DAY NIGHT FEVER

You're Invited!

FRIDAY, APRIL 14TH, 7 PM

The Saltzman Estate
363 Magnolia Tree Lane

PLEASE RSVP BY APRIL 5TH
to
saltzmanpepper@gmail.com

Invitation design by PARTY ON THE SQUARE

Season 2, Episode 3

CAM:
Our friend Pepper loves to throw theme parties.

MITCHELL:
Yes, he does, and this weekend is his first annual "Oscar Wilde and Crazy Brunch."

CAM:
We're still recovering from his "Studio 54th of July" barbecue. They were fun at first . . .

MITCHELL:
. . . Cam, can we just— can we please cancel?

CAM:
I wish we could, but you know, he's still mad at us for missing Passover.

MITCHELL:
Oh, right. Seder-Day Night Fever.

Season 3, Episode 2

MITCHELL:

Lily, honey, did Daddy pick you up early from preschool today?

LILY:

No.

CAM:

Case closed.

LILY:

We didn't go.

MITCHELL:

Case opened.

LILY:

We went shopping.

CAM:

That's enough.

LILY:

We bought matchy hats.

cam's | vegetarian rice-paper rolls *with* nuoc cham

Serves 8

2 ounces uncooked rice vermicelli

8 ounces sliced shiitake mushroom caps

2 tablespoons vegetable oil

Kosher salt and freshly ground black pepper

1 cup julienned carrots

¼ cup packed fresh basil leaves

¼ cup packed fresh mint leaves

¼ cup packed fresh cilantro leaves

8 (6-inch) rice paper sheets, plus more in case of tearing

Nuoc Cham (recipe follows)

1 Put the rice noodles in a large bowl; cover with boiling water and let stand for 8 minutes, until pliable. Drain, then rinse under cold running water until cool. Drain and squeeze dry. Return the noodles to the bowl.

2 In a large skillet, sauté the shiitakes in the oil over high heat until softened and lightly browned, about 8 minutes. Season with salt and pepper and let cool. Transfer to the bowl with the noodles, along with the carrot, basil, mint, and cilantro, and toss gently.

3 Fill a pie plate with cold water. Working with one rice paper sheet at a time, dip it into the water and let sit for 30 seconds. Transfer the rice paper to a work surface and let sit until pliable, about 30 seconds longer. Put about ½ loose cup of the filling on the lower half of the rice paper and roll up into a tight cylinder, tucking in the sides as you roll. Transfer to a platter and cover with a damp paper towel. Repeat with the remaining rice paper sheets and filling. Cut each in half and serve with the Nuoc Cham.

nuoc cham

Makes about ½ cup

¼ **cup Vietnamese fish sauce**

2 **tablespoons fresh lime juice**

2 **tablespoons light brown sugar**

1 **Thai bird chili (or any other very hot fresh chili), thinly sliced**

2 **tablespoons chopped fresh cilantro**

1 In a bowl, combine all of the ingredients with 2 tablespoons water and stir until the sugar is dissolved.

"Do we spend a lot of time together? Yes.
Do we have a special bond? Absolutely. But do I
coddle her more than any other loving parent?

It's possible."

—— C A M ——

mitchell's | smoked salmon canapés

Makes 34

4 ounces cream cheese, softened

¼ cup sour cream

1 tablespoon honey

½ teaspoon freshly ground black
   pepper, plus more for garnish

¼ teaspoon kosher salt

4 ounces sliced rye or
   pumpernickel bread

2 (4-ounce) packages thinly sliced
   smoked salmon

2 medium cucumbers

1 small red onion, minced

Fresh dill sprigs

1 Combine the cream cheese, sour cream, honey, pepper, and salt in a bowl; beat at low speed with an electric mixer until smooth.

2 Cut each bread slice in half diagonally. Separate the salmon slices and cut into 34 strips. Spread ½ teaspoon of the cream cheese mixture onto each bread triangle. Using a vegetable peeler, cut the cucumbers into 34 thin slices. Roll a cucumber slice inside each piece of salmon; place over the cream cheese spread on the bread triangles. Dollop ½ teaspoon of the cream cheese mixture over the salmon. Sprinkle with the onion and a little more pepper; garnish with dill and serve immediately.

TIP: If you like more bite, coarsely crack the peppercorns rather than grinding them.

Season 2, Episode 18

MITCHELL:
Saturday night we're having dinner with Pepper, Longinus, and Crispin.

CAM:
They're our gay friends.

MITCHELL:
I think that was clear. I've been spending a lot of time with a lot of straight people lately, and, darlin', I need a night with my homies.

CAM:
You mean homos.

HOW TO GET RID OF
annoying houseguests

In the wise words of Gloria Delgado-Pritchett: "Houseguests start to stink after three days, much like dead bodies." No one knows that better than Cam and Mitchell, who have gotten themselves into some tricky pickles with visitors in their home over the years. If you ever find yourself with unwanted company, rely on these handy tips.

BARRY, THE HOMELESS REIKI MASTER

BRENDA, THE DIVORCED COWORKER

DYLAN, THE NIECE'S EX-BOYFRIEND

MITCHELL & CAM, THE SON & SON-IN-LAW

TIP 1	**Call the cops.**

When you discover that your upstairs neighbor is actually a homeless Reiki master who is squatting in your daughter's princess castle, phoning the police is probably warranted. Cam and Mitchell learned this lesson the hard way when they caught Barry in their hot tub, but they overlooked his offense because he was so attractive. Don't make the same mistake; trespassing is trespassing, no matter how toned your vagabond's abs are.

TIP 2	**Make your guests as uncomfortable as possible.**

When Mitchell's recently divorced coworker Brenda moved in with him temporarily, Cam and Mitchell tried to force her to sleep on a tiny love seat. Brenda, however, opted for the brand-new solid white designer couch that—up until that point—only the white cat had been allowed to sit on. To keep her from drooling on the throw pillows, Cam and Mitchell bundled her up like a burrito once she was asleep.

If you accidentally get so drunk at your own Valentine's Day cocktail party that you dye your cat red and invite your niece's ex-boyfriend to live with you, you might need reinforcements when you sober up and are forced to kick him out. Cam and Mitchell left it to Lily to tell Dylan, "You can't live here! It's weird! You're a big boy!"

Cam and Mitchell drove Gloria and Jay crazy when they moved in while their house was being fumigated. Mitchell got into a huge fight with his dad about his insensitive lawyer jokes. Cam got into a diva-style brawl with Gloria about the way she mothered Lily. Remember the patience of your former hosts when annoying houseguests are testing your own.

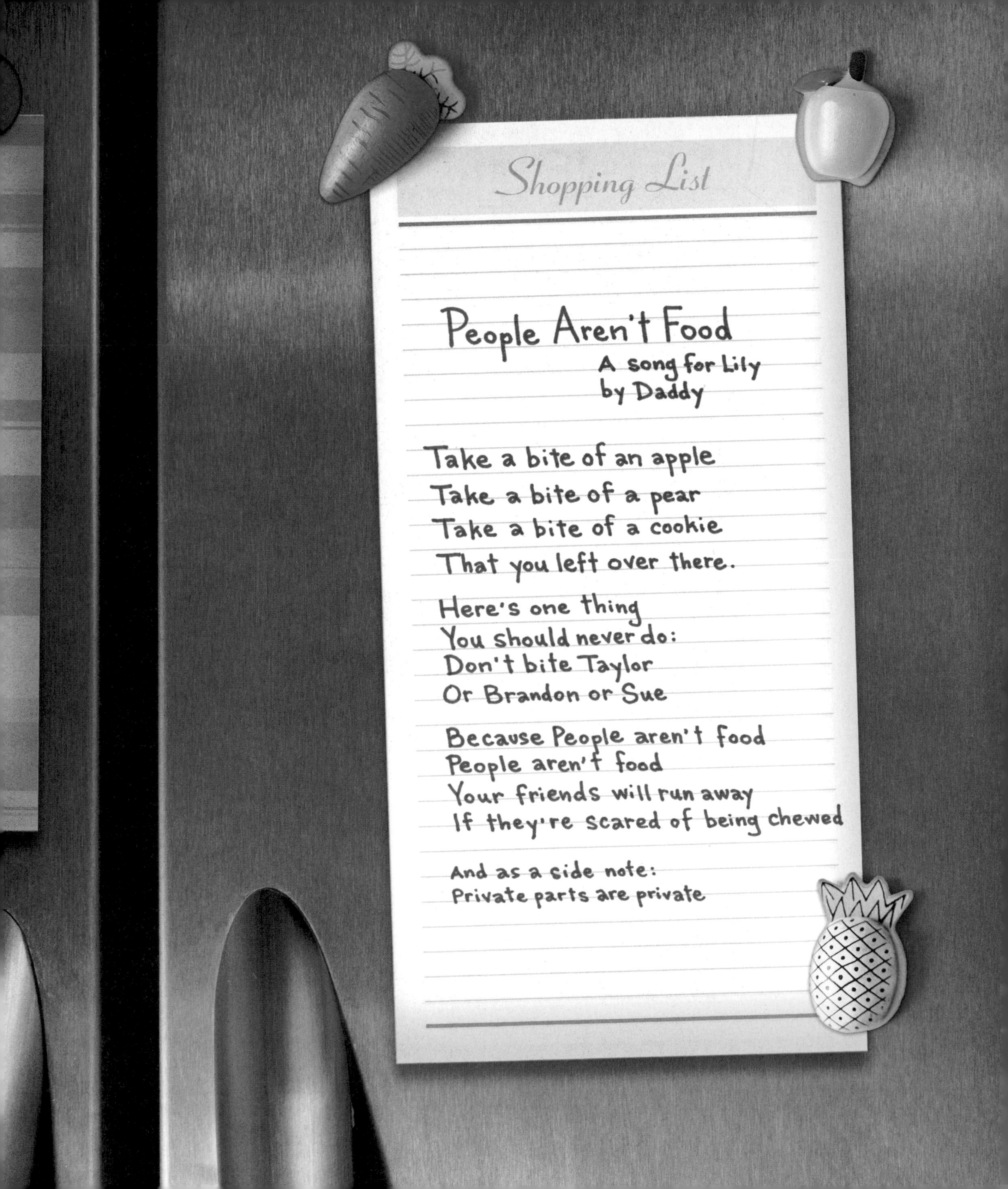

People Aren't Food

A song for Lily
by Daddy

Take a bite of an apple
Take a bite of a pear
Take a bite of a cookie
That you left over there.

Here's one thing
You should never do:
Don't bite Taylor
Or Brandon or Sue

Because People aren't food
People aren't food
Your friends will run away
If they're scared of being chewed

And as a side note:
Private parts are private

lily's | pot stickers

Makes 24 pot stickers; serves 6

¼ cup plum sauce

2 tablespoons low-sodium soy sauce

3 green onions

1 tablespoon chopped peeled fresh ginger

2 garlic cloves

⅓ cup loosely packed fresh cilantro leaves

2 (¾-inch-thick) center-cut boneless pork loin chops

1 large egg, separated

¼ teaspoon kosher salt

¼ teaspoon crushed red pepper

24 wonton wrappers

2 teaspoons sesame oil

1 (14-ounce) can low-sodium chicken broth

1 Combine the plum sauce and soy sauce in a small bowl; stir well. Cover and chill.

2 Put the green onions, ginger, garlic, and cilantro in a food processor; pulse ten times or until the mixture is finely chopped. Transfer the mixture to a large bowl.

3 Trim the fat from the pork; cut the pork into thin slices. Put the pork in the food processor; pulse until finely ground. Add the pork to the green onion mixture. Stir in the egg yolk, salt, and crushed red pepper until thoroughly combined.

4 Working with one wonton wrapper at a time (cover the remaining wrappers with a damp towel to keep them from drying out), spoon 1 rounded teaspoon of the pork mixture onto the center of the wrapper. Moisten the edges of the dough with beaten egg white, and bring two opposite corners together. Pinch the edges together to seal, forming a triangle. Place the pot sticker on a platter; cover loosely with a damp towel to keep it from drying out. Repeat with the remaining pork mixture and wonton wrappers.

5 Heat 1 teaspoon of the sesame oil in a large nonstick skillet over medium-low heat. Arrange half of the pot stickers in the pan. Cook for 3 minutes on each side or until lightly browned. Remove from the pan; set aside. Repeat with the remaining sesame oil and pot stickers.

6 Return all the pot stickers to the pan; add the broth. Bring to a boil. Cover, reduce the heat, and simmer for 3 minutes. Remove the pot stickers from the pan using a slotted spoon; serve immediately with the plum sauce mixture.

Season 2, Episode 10

MITCHELL:
Okay, I don't get it. Why is she biting? Lily, why are you biting?

CAM:
She's not biting. She's teething.

MITCHELL:
On people. All right, if she starts biting her playdates, she's gonna be a pariah.

CAM:
Try piranha.

MITCHELL:
Really, Cam?

CAM:
It was right there.

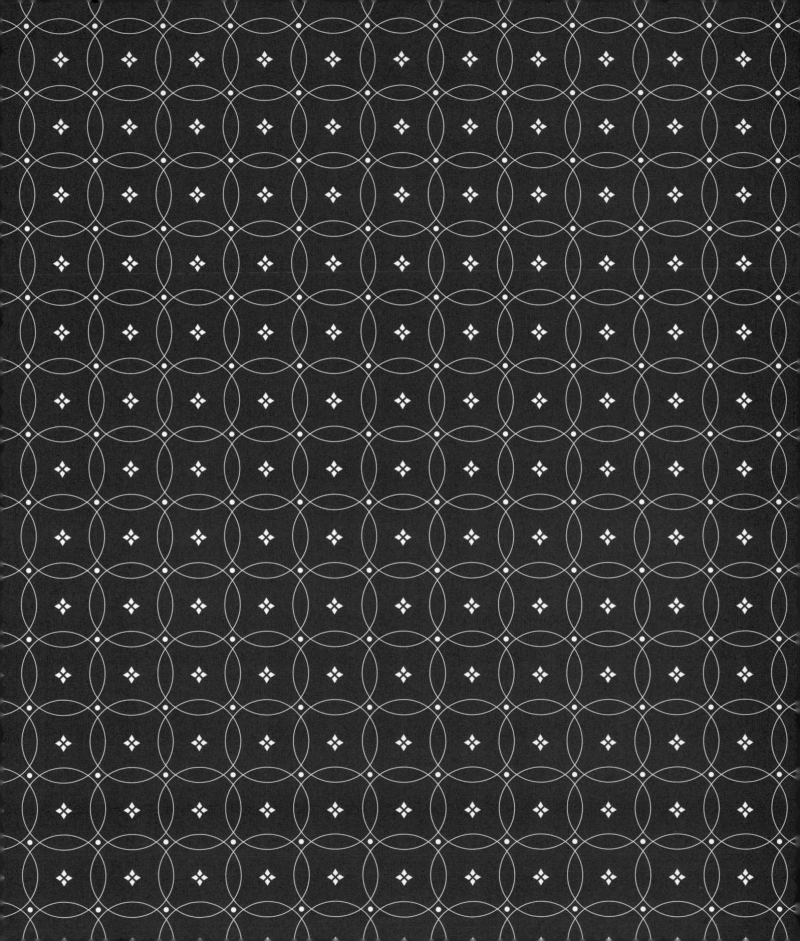

SALADS, SOUPS, *and* SANDWICHES

skip woosnum's | wedge salad

Serves 6

¾ cup mayonnaise

¼ cup evaporated milk or buttermilk

1 tablespoon fresh lemon juice

1 (4-ounce) package crumbled blue cheese

1 head iceberg lettuce

2 slices bacon, cooked and crumbled

1½ cups chopped tomatoes

1 Combine the mayonnaise, evaporated milk, and lemon juice in a small bowl; stir in the blue cheese.

2 Remove the outer leaves from the lettuce and discard. Rinse the lettuce under cold running water; drain well. Remove the core. Cut lettuce into 6 wedges and place them on individual serving plates. Top each wedge evenly with ¼ cup of the dressing, 1 teaspoon bacon, and ¼ cup tomato. Serve immediately.

Season 2, Episode 16

CLAIRE:

Since I met him, I've been trying to get Phil to try a wedge salad. The minute that Skip Woosnum— whom he doesn't even like—suggests it, Phil thinks it's the best thing ever, and he does this with everything. He does it with books, movies, with TV. He listens to everybody's opinion but mine, and it drives me crazy.

"Wedge salad. You gotta try it."

— PHIL —

claire's | white bean *and* tomato salad

Serves 4

1 (15-ounce) can navy beans,
  drained and rinsed

1 large tomato, chopped

¼ cup prepared balsamic
  vinaigrette

Bibb lettuce leaves

Freshly ground black pepper
  (optional)

1 Combine the beans and tomato in a medium bowl. Add the vinaigrette, stirring to coat. Divide the lettuce leaves among individual serving plates. Spoon the bean mixture over the lettuce. Sprinkle with pepper, if desired. Serve immediately.

TIP: Toss the beans and tomatoes in a to-go container; wrap the chilled leaves in a damp paper towel and stick them in a separate container; and pack it away for a healthy on-the-go lunch.

Season 5, Episode 3

CLAIRE:

I'm stretched a little thin today, so I need you to do the grocery shopping, check in on the kids, and maybe clean up those branches in the front yard.

PHIL:

Done and done.

CLAIRE:

Is that an expression, or did you really only remember two of the things I said?

PHIL:

The second.

claire's | arugula salad *with* prosciutto *and* pears

Serves 4

2 (5-ounce) bags arugula

2 red pears, cored and cut lengthwise into ¼-inch-thick slices

4 thin slices (about 2 ounces) prosciutto, cut crosswise into strips

¾ cup (about 3 ounces) shaved Parmesan cheese

¼ cup walnut halves, toasted (see Note)

3 tablespoons white wine vinegar

2 tablespoons extra-virgin olive oil

¼ teaspoon kosher salt

⅛ teaspoon freshly ground black pepper

1 Combine the arugula, pears, prosciutto, cheese, and walnuts in a large bowl.

2 Combine the vinegar, oil, salt, and pepper in a small bowl, stirring with a whisk. Drizzle over the salad and toss gently to coat. Serve immediately.

NOTE: Toast the walnut halves quickly in a dry skillet over medium-high heat. Stir frequently, and remove them from the heat as soon as you begin to smell that wonderful nutty aroma.

Season 2, Episode 21

CLAIRE:

Okay, I don't want you to judge me, but I have to say. Sometimes I wanna punch my kids.

GLORIA:

You don't mean that.

CLAIRE:

No, I do. I do. The last time they were horrible the way they were today, they happened to be all lined up. And I couldn't help but think if I hit just one of 'em the rest would go down like dominoes.

GLORIA:

Jeez.

CLAIRE:

I know, that would rob me of the pleasure of hitting each one individually, but . . .

WHICH
modern family parent
ARE YOU?

Whether it's peer-enting or helicopter mom-ing, every parent on *Modern Family* has a different parenting style. Follow the flowchart below to find out which *Modern Family* parent you are.

START

You accidentally lock your kid in the car. What do you do?

Remain calm and call OnStar.

Panic! Yell! Maybe break one of the windows!

Your daughter wants to wear a tiara to a fancy event. Do you:

Reason with her. Tiaras are for Halloween.

Let her. She's a princess. Of course she can wear a tiara.

What do you do when your kid tells you he wants to learn to ride a bike?

Wrap him up in head-to-toe protective gear.

Try to convince him to help you build a time machine with bike parts instead.

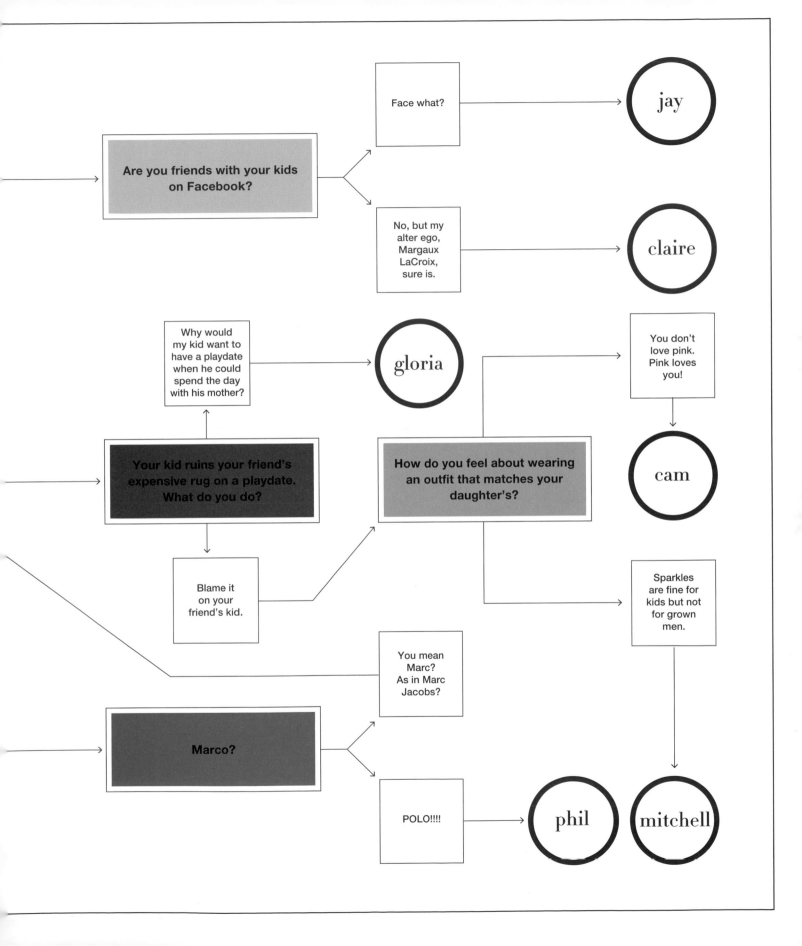

Are you friends with your kids on Facebook?

Face what? → jay

No, but my alter ego, Margaux LaCroix, sure is. → claire

Why would my kid want to have a playdate when he could spend the day with his mother? → gloria

Your kid ruins your friend's expensive rug on a playdate. What do you do?

Blame it on your friend's kid.

How do you feel about wearing an outfit that matches your daughter's?

You don't love pink. Pink loves you! → cam

Sparkles are fine for kids but not for grown men. → mitchell

You mean Marc? As in Marc Jacobs?

Marco?

POLO!!!! → phil

CAM:

Hey, Daddy! How was the farmers' market?

MITCHELL:

Well, it was great, but guess what the new spinach is?

CAM:

Um, radicchio?

MITCHELL:

Kale.

CAM:

No.

MITCHELL:

I know, I was just as blown away as you are.

mitchell's | kale caesar salad

Serves 4

- **2 slices (¾ inch thick) sourdough bread, roughly torn into ¾-inch pieces**
- **6 tablespoons extra-virgin olive oil**
- **1 large bunch Tuscan (lacinato) kale (1 pound), stems and inner ribs removed, leaves chopped**
- **Sea salt**

- **3 anchovy fillets, mashed**
- **1 small garlic clove, smashed**
- **¼ cup mayonnaise**
- **2 tablespoons fresh lemon juice**
- **½ cup freshly grated Parmesan cheese**
- **Freshly ground black pepper**

1 Preheat the oven to 350°F. In a large bowl, toss the bread with 3 table-spoons of the oil. Spread it out on a sturdy baking sheet and toast, stirring occasionally, until golden and crisp, 8 to 10 minutes.

2 Put the kale in the bowl and season lightly with salt. Using your hands, squeeze the leaves gently to wilt them slightly.

3 In another bowl, mash the anchovies with the garlic and a pinch of salt to a smooth paste. Whisk in the mayonnaise and lemon juice and the remaining 3 tablespoons oil. Fold in half of the cheese, and season generously with pepper. Pour the dressing over the kale and toss to coat. Add the croutons, toss again, and transfer to plates. Sprinkle with the remaining cheese and serve immediately.

andy's | red quinoa salad

Serves 4

1 cup uncooked red quinoa

⅓ cup extra-virgin olive oil

2 tablespoons red wine vinegar

1½ teaspoons finely minced shallot

¼ teaspoon kosher salt

¼ teaspoon freshly ground black pepper

2 cups (½-inch) diced seeded tomatoes

½ cup (½-inch) diced seeded cucumber

3 tablespoons chopped fresh mint

1 tablespoon chopped fresh oregano

1 (15-ounce) can chickpeas (garbanzo beans), rinsed and drained

½ cup (2 ounces) crumbled feta cheese

4 lemon wedges

1 Cook the quinoa according to the package directions, omitting salt and fat. Drain and put in a large bowl. Let cool for 1 hour.

2 While the quinoa cools, combine the oil, vinegar, shallot, salt, and pepper in a small bowl, stirring with a whisk. Let the dressing stand for 20 minutes.

3 Add the dressing, tomatoes, cucumber, mint, oregano, and chickpeas to the quinoa; toss well. Add the cheese and toss gently. Serve with the lemon wedges.

KIDS CAN HELP!

With a child-safe knife, kids can chop the tomatoes and cucumber. They can also crumble the feta.

Season 5, Episode 6

ANDY:
I'm kind of a chef, too. Here, try this.

GLORIA, AFTER TAKING A BITE:
Mmm!

ANDY:
It's quinoa. You actually burn calories while eating it—

GLORIA:
So, Andy, tell me, are you really happy with that Joan?

"My mission is to make all of your lives
healthier and happier."

—ANDY

jay's | couscous salad

Serves 4

½ (16-ounce) package frozen stir-fry vegetables with broccoli

1 (10-ounce) package garlic-flavored couscous

4 tablespoons Caesar salad dressing

1 (10-ounce) package fresh spinach

½ cup (2 ounces) crumbled feta cheese

1 Combine vegetables, 1¼ cups water, and the seasoning packet from the couscous in a large saucepan; bring to a boil. Add the couscous, stirring well. Remove from the heat; cover and let stand for 5 minutes or until the liquid is absorbed. Stir in 1 tablespoon of the dressing.

2 While the couscous stands, remove and discard the stems from the spinach. Wash the spinach, and pat it dry with paper towels. Chop the spinach and put it in a large bowl. Drizzle the remaining 3 tablespoons of the dressing over the spinach and toss well. Spoon the couscous mixture over the spinach and sprinkle with the cheese. Serve immediately.

Season 1, Episode 15

GLORIA:

I love you. You're my valentine.

JAY:

For now, but what about when I'm eighty? And I'm in a wheelchair on oxygen. You still gonna want me?

GLORIA:

Do you think I'm so shallow that I'm gonna leave you when you're old? What if I gained a hundred pounds? You gonna leave me then?

JAY:

No.

GLORIA:

What's with the pause?

JAY:

Well, it's not exactly fair. I mean, I have to get old, you don't have to get fat.

gloria's | tomato *and* avocado salad

Serves 2 to 4

- 2 **vine-ripened tomatoes, thinly sliced**
- 2 **Hass avocados, thinly sliced**
- 1 **seedless cucumber, thinly sliced**
- 1 **small red onion, thinly sliced**
- 2 **tablespoons white wine vinegar**

- 2 **tablespoons fresh lime juice**
- 6 **tablespoons extra-virgin olive oil**
- **Kosher salt and freshly ground black pepper**
- 2 **tablespoons chopped fresh cilantro**

1 Arrange the tomatoes, avocados, cucumber, and onion on a platter. In a small bowl, whisk the vinegar with the lime juice and oil and season with salt and pepper. Drizzle the dressing over the salad and garnish with cilantro. Serve immediately.

See photo on following spread

PROPERTY OF
CITY OF LOS ANGELES, CA
VEHICLE FOR HIRE
DRIVER'S PERMIT

DRIVER NAME: GLORIA DELGADO

PERMIT # 3553

DRIVER SIGNATURE

ISSUED: 09/07/2005
EXPIRES: 09/07/2006

ISSUED BY:
DEPARTMENT OF TRANSPORTATION BY:
This license is non-transferrable.

GLORIA, LOOKING AT HER AND MANNY'S COLLECTION OF LUCKY PENNIES:
Ay, look at this one, the green one. The one we found on the floor of my taxi.

JAY:
Your taxi?

GLORIA:
Yes. Before I had somebody running my life for me, I used to drive a taxi at night. Manny would sleep in the seat next to me. One time, I had to hit the brakes so hard that he fell into the floor, and he found the penny.

Season 1, Episode 13

MANNY, TO CAMERA:
Her name is Whitney. I met her in an online book club. We both like vampire fiction and the romance of eternal life.

GLORIA, TO CAMERA:
I think it's adorable that Manny has a "date." He even picked out the lunch menu. Grilled cheese sandwiches and tomato soup. Tomato soup because, you know, that tomato soup looks like the blood and the vampires like to eat the blood. And then he wants me to take them out for ice cream, well, because, Manny likes ice cream.

gloria *and* manny's | tomato soup *and* grilled cheese

Serves 3

- **2 tablespoons unsalted butter, plus 1 tablespoon softened**
- **1 cup chopped onion**
- **2 tablespoons minced fresh tarragon (optional)**
- **½ teaspoon sugar**
- **1 garlic clove, chopped**
- **2 (28-ounce) cans Italian-style whole tomatoes**

- **3 cups low-sodium organic vegetable broth**
- **3 tablespoons tomato paste**
- **½ cup half-and-half**
- **½ cup heavy cream**
- **6 slices country white bread**
- **6 slices American cheese**

1 Melt 2 tablespoons of the butter in a Dutch oven over medium heat. Add the onion; cook for 10 minutes, stirring occasionally. Add the tarragon if desired, sugar, and garlic; sauté for 2 minutes. Add the tomatoes and the juice from one of the cans (reserve the juice of the other can for another use), broth, and tomato paste. Increase the heat to medium-high and bring to a boil; partially cover, reduce the heat to medium-low, and simmer for 30 minutes.

2 Remove from the heat; let cool for 5 minutes. Put half of the soup mixture in a blender; process until smooth. Return the soup to a clean saucepan. Repeat with the remaining soup mixture. Add the half-and-half and cream, stirring with a whisk over low heat. Set aside; keep warm.

3 While the soup simmers, place 3 bread slices on a work surface; arrange 2 cheese slices on each of the 3 bread slices. Top with the remaining 3 bread slices. Spread softened butter on the outsides of the sandwiches. Heat a large nonstick skillet over medium heat. Add the

sandwiches to the pan; cook for 4 minutes or until lightly browned. Turn the sandwiches over; cook for 2 minutes or until the cheese melts. Cut each sandwich in half diagonally.

4 Ladle the soup into bowls; serve with the sandwiches.

TIP: Go ahead and use processed cheese—the nostalgia factor is worth it.

See photo on previous spread

"The tomato soup looks like the blood,
and the vampires like to eat the blood."

—GLORIA

cam *and* mitchell's | butternut squash bisque

Serves 4 to 6 as a starter, or more as an hors d'oeuvre

- 1 **small butternut squash (about 1 pound)**
- 1 **stalk celery, sliced**
- 1¾ **cups low-sodium chicken broth**
- 2 **cups peeled, sliced Rome apple**
- ¾ **cup peeled, sliced potato**
- ¾ **cup sliced onion**
- ⅓ **cup sliced carrot**
- ¼ **teaspoon dried oregano**
- ¼ **teaspoon dried rosemary**
- ¼ **cup milk**
- **Toasted pepitas (hulled pumpkin seeds)**
- **Cracked black pepper**

1 Peel the squash; cut it in half and remove the seeds. Slice each half crosswise. Combine the squash, celery, broth, apple, potato, onion, carrot, oregano, and rosemary in a Dutch oven; bring to a boil. Cover, reduce the heat, and simmer for 20 to 30 minutes or until tender.

2 Working in batches, process the mixture in a blender until smooth. Return the puree to the Dutch oven and stir in the milk. Cook over low heat, stirring constantly, until thoroughly heated. Ladle into serving bowls, garnish each serving with a few pepitas and a pinch of cracked pepper, and serve hot.

Season 5, Episode 6

MITCHELL:
We're getting married in seven months.

CAM:
Or eight months.

MITCHELL:
I don't like getting married in April.

CAM:
Well, I don't like sweating in May.

mitchell's | pb & j (pear, brie, *and* jambon) tartines

Serves 3, or more as an appetizer or snack

6 slices bakery white bread

2 tablespoons unsalted butter, melted

½ cup pear preserves or chutney

2 tablespoons grainy Dijon mustard

¼ teaspoon smoked paprika or cayenne

Pinch of kosher salt

8 ounces Brie, with rind, thinly sliced

4 ounces sliced Serrano ham or prosciutto

½ red Bartlett pear, cored and thinly sliced

1 Preheat the oven to 350°F.

2 Brush the bread with the butter and arrange it on a baking sheet. Toast until golden and crisp, turning each slice once, about 10 minutes. Turn on the broiler.

3 In a bowl, combine the preserves, mustard, paprika, and salt and spread it on the toast. Top with the Brie and broil until melted. Top with the ham and pear and serve warm.

TIP: Pear, Brie, and jambon is a delightful treat in a brown-bag lunch, but it also works as a fancy-party finger food. Just cut each toast in half on the diagonal.

Season 2, Episode 19

CAM:

And as the music swells, we reveal our letters spelling "We Love the World." Powerful stuff. And then the majestic Franklin Middle School insignia will drop into position . . . if Reuben ever finishes painting it.

(TO REUBEN)

It's not the Sistine Chapel, Reuben.

MITCHELL:

Surprise! Hi, your supportive boyfriend dropped by to bring you a snack. PB & J.

CAM:

Pear, Brie, and jambon. My favorite! Okay, people, let's take five! A true five.

the jay pritchett

Serves 2

FOR THE ANCHOVY AIOLI:

1 garlic clove, mashed

Pinch of kosher salt

2 anchovy fillets, chopped

2 tablespoons red wine vinegar

½ cup mayonnaise

2 tablespoons extra-virgin olive oil

FOR THE SANDWICHES:

6 slices whole-grain bakery bread, lightly toasted

¼ cup jarred piquillo peppers or roasted red peppers, cut into thin strips

6 ounces thinly sliced turkey

2 cups baby arugula or shredded lettuce

8 slices crisp-cooked bacon

1 Make the anchovy aioli: In a medium bowl, using a spoon, mash the garlic, salt, and anchovy to a paste. Whisk in the vinegar, then the mayonnaise. Gradually whisk in the oil.

2 Make the sandwiches: Arrange two of the slices of toast on a work surface and spread each with 1 tablespoon of the aioli. Arrange the roasted peppers, followed by the turkey and half of the arugula, on top of the aioli. Arrange two more slices of toast on a work surface and spread each with 1 tablespoon of the aioli. Top with the bacon and remaining arugula. Place them on top of the first slices. Spread each of the two remaining slices of toast with 1 tablespoon of the aioli. Place, face down, on the sandwich and press lightly to compact.

3 Poke two skewers in each sandwich, cut them in half down the middle, and serve.

Season 3, Episode 23

GLORIA, LOOKING AT THE MENU:
They named you after a sandwich?

JAY:
No, they named a sandwich after me.

GLORIA:
Turkey, bacon, Swiss cheese, red peppers, anchovies on wheat?

JAY:
Most people stop after salty bacon, but I doubled down with the anchovies.

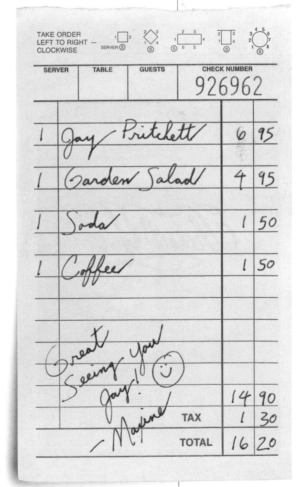

Season 5, Episode 22

MANNY:

Have you ever really examined a jar of pickles, Jay? It's like a swamp in there. I'll pass.

GLORIA:

What happened?

JAY:

I made him a beautiful sandwich, and he won't eat it.

GLORIA:

Yeah, 'cause it had pickles on it. Joe is taking a nap. I'm gonna go to the dry cleaners.

MANNY:

Well, if you're passing a sushi restaurant—

JAY:

She's not. I've never heard of anyone not liking pickles.

GLORIA:

Aw, big day for you, then.

MANNY:

I'm just gonna make myself a grilled cheese. I think I saw some Gruyère in there. Do we have any fig?

manny's | prosciutto, gruyère, and fig panini

Serves 4

8 slices crusty Chicago-style Italian bread

4 ounces very thinly sliced prosciutto

1¼ cups (4 ounces) shredded Gruyère cheese

½ cup baby arugula leaves

4 tablespoons fig preserves

Olive oil–flavored cooking spray

1 Preheat a panini grill.

2 Top each of 4 bread slices evenly with prosciutto, cheese, and arugula. Spread 1 tablespoon of the fig preserves evenly over one side of each of the remaining 4 bread slices; close the sandwiches. Coat the outsides of sandwiches with cooking spray. Place the sandwiches on the panini grill; cook for 3 to 4 minutes, until golden and the cheese is melted. Cut the panini in half before serving, if desired.

TIP: If you don't have a panini grill, make this sandwich grilled-cheese style, on a griddle over medium heat, pressing down on the sandwiches with a sturdy spatula or a heavy skillet to flatten them; turn the sandwiches over halfway through to brown the other side.

claire's | crunchy surprise sandwich

Serves 4

½ **cup mayonnaise**

3 **tablespoons chopped fresh cilantro**

1 **scallion, finely chopped**

2 **tablespoons fresh lime juice**

Kosher salt and freshly ground black pepper

3 **cups shredded rotisserie chicken meat (about 12 ounces)**

8 **slices bakery-style white or whole-grain bread**

2 **cups spicy flavored potato chips, such as sriracha or spicy Thai**

1 In a bowl, combine the mayonnaise with the cilantro, scallion, and lime juice and season with salt and pepper. Add the chicken and fold to combine. Divide the chicken salad among 4 slices of bread. Top with the potato chips, close the sandwiches, and press lightly. Cut each in half and serve.

Season 2, Episode 8

LUKE:

You do fun stuff. You put that potato chip in my sandwich. That was a crunchy surprise.

CLAIRE:

That was your dad. Everything fun is your dad. Second Christmas, Italian accent night . . .

claire's | chicken *and* vegetable garden wraps

Season 3, Episode 2

PHIL:

Your word against mine.
It's one of those things
we'll just never know.
Like what really happened
to the *Titanic*.

CLAIRE:

It hit an iceberg.

PHIL:

Maybe.

Serves 6

1½ (6-ounce) packages grilled chicken breast strips, diced

⅔ cup thinly sliced red bell pepper

½ cup thinly sliced celery

½ cup vertically sliced red onion

½ cup frozen petite green peas

½ cup light ranch dressing

⅓ cup (about 1½ ounces) crumbled blue cheese

4 cups chopped romaine lettuce

6 (8-inch) flour tortillas

1 Stir together the chicken, bell pepper, celery, onion, peas, dressing, and cheese in a medium bowl.

2 Spoon about ⅔ cup each of the lettuce and the chicken mixture onto the center of each tortilla; fold the edges of the tortilla over the filling. Roll up the tortillas and secure with wooden picks; wrap in waxed paper. Chill in the refrigerator. Cut diagonally in half; carefully remove wooden picks. Serve cold.

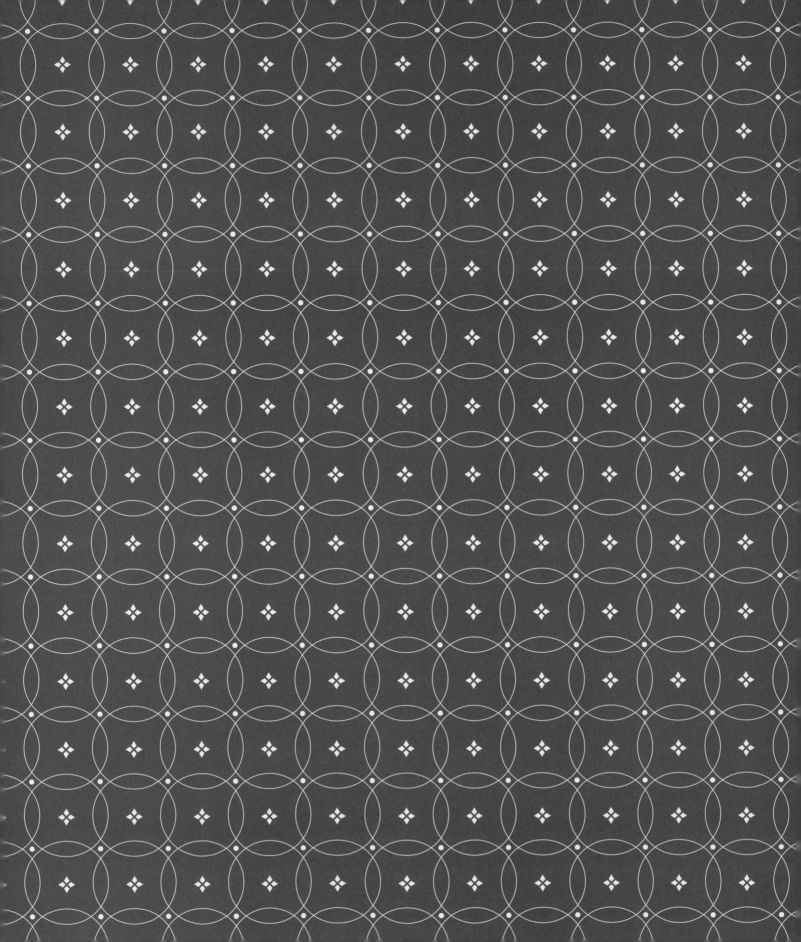

SIDES

Season 5, Episode 5

MITCHELL:

All right, one of us has to change. We look like twin toddlers at church.

CAM:

Yeah, tell me about it. And this place we're going is supposed to be super hip. We're probably gonna run into someone. And come on. I don't have that many outfits.

MITCHELL:

My clothes take up exactly one-quarter of the closet.

CAM:

That's not fair. My clothes are bigger than yours.

MITCHELL:

All right, I hate to play this card, but I was dressed first. So . . .

CAM:

Oh, that is silly. Lily, it's time to play "Who Wore It Best?"

mitchell's | tomatoes *with* green onions *and* basil

Serves 2

- 1½ teaspoons olive oil
- 1 pint grape tomatoes or cherry tomatoes
- 1½ tablespoons thinly sliced green onions
- 1 tablespoon minced fresh basil
- 2 teaspoons balsamic vinegar
- ¼ teaspoon kosher salt
- ⅛ teaspoon freshly ground black pepper

1 Heat the oil in a large nonstick skillet over medium-high heat. Add the tomatoes; sauté for 1 to 2 minutes or until the tomatoes are heated through. Remove from the heat and stir in all the remaining ingredients; toss gently. Serve immediately.

Also see photo on page 179

cam's | kale salad greens

Serves 8 to 10

1 **(8-ounce) smoked ham hock**

2 **medium onions, peeled and quartered**

1 **small hot red pepper**

2 **bunches (about 3 pounds) kale**

1 Wash the ham hock and place it in an 8-quart Dutch oven. Add the onions, red pepper, and 2 quarts water; bring to a boil. Reduce the heat; simmer for 2 hours or until the meat is tender.

2 Check the kale carefully; remove any pulpy stems and discolored spots on leaves. Wash the kale thoroughly; drain well. Chop the kale leaves. Add the kale to the Dutch oven; bring to a boil. Cover, reduce the heat, and simmer for 2 hours or until the kale is tender. Remove the red pepper; discard. Spoon the kale into a serving dish and serve hot.

NOTE: Smoked ham hocks (and salt pork, which you'll need for the rutabagas opposite) give long-cooked vegetables that typical Southern-style lusciousness. Look for both of these delicious cured products in the farthest corner of the grocery store meat case, near the sausages and fresh pork cuts, or in the freezer section with random meats and oddities.

See photo on page 178

Season 4, Episode 9

CAM:

Guess what they are cutting down at the park today?

MITCHELL:

A tree.

CAM:

Yes. How did you know that?

MITCHELL:

I played a hunch.

CAM:

Not just any tree, Tree-ona Elmsly.

MITCHELL:

Oh, no. That's terrible. That's our picnic tree.

LILY:

It's a nightmare.

MITCHELL:

Well, someone's picked up her daddy's gift for hyperbole.

cam's | southern-cooked rutabagas

Serves 4 to 6

- 1 (2-pound) rutabaga, peeled and cubed
- ¼ pound salt pork, rinsed and sliced
- 1 teaspoon sugar
- ½ teaspoon kosher salt
- ⅛ teaspoon freshly ground black pepper, plus more for serving

1. Combine the rutabaga, 3 cups water, the salt pork, sugar, and salt in a Dutch oven. Bring to a boil. Reduce the heat; simmer, uncovered, for 35 minutes or until the rutabaga is tender. Drain. Remove the salt pork; discard.

2. Add the pepper to the rutabaga; mash to the desired consistency. Sprinkle with additional pepper. Serve hot.

See photo on page 178

See photo on page 178

Season 6, Episode 7

ANNE GIBBS:
Has anyone ever approached you for a news segment?

CAM:
On me?! Oh, my gosh. No. I don't . . . I don't think I'm interesting enough to do a news segment on. I mean, what would a reporter even say about me? That I'm a high school football coach with an undefeated record who's tackling stereotypes, that on my team, prejudice is considered out of bounds, that we're blitzing bigotry, kicking intolerance, and beating—

MITCHELL:
Metaphors to death?

WEEKLY SAVER   Page 9

Gay Coach Breaks Records and Stereotypes

By Joanna Marple

A high school football coach led his team to an unexpected victory last night and became the first freshman Dolphin coach ever to win three games in his first season. "Even local coaching legends Burt LeVoisier, Red Stagg, Duckie Pond had only ever won two games in their first season," said Coach Cameron Tucker, "so this was a really huge accomplishment for us."

With just twelve seconds left and a six-point deficit, freshman Matt Woodson pulled off a classic "triple gull-wing" play, faking left and right and then faking *faking* right to score the game-winning touchdown. When asked if he felt like luck had played a part in his team's victory, Tucker responded with the classic adage: "Good coaches don't need luck. We make luck."

Coach Tucker isn't just a leader on the field, he has also been praised for his unabashed status as an openly gay football coach. "I am standing here boldly abolishing gay stereotypes," said Tucker. "It feels so great. I feel like the Belle of the Football."

See "GAY COACH" page 14

"I feel like the Belle of the Football."
—COACH CAMERON TUCKER

gloria's | cilantro-lime rice

Makes about 3½ cups; serves 6

½ teaspoon canola oil

½ cup chopped onion

1 cup jasmine or other long-grain rice

1½ cups low-sodium chicken broth

2 tablespoons fresh lime juice

¼ cup coarsely chopped fresh cilantro

1 Heat a medium saucepan over medium heat. Add the oil; swirl to coat. Add the onion; cook for 5 minutes or until tender, stirring frequently. Stir in the rice, broth, and 1 tablespoon of the lime juice. Bring to a boil; reduce the heat, cover, and simmer for 15 minutes or until the rice is tender and the liquid is absorbed. Remove from the heat. Add the remaining 1 tablespoon lime juice and the cilantro; fluff with a fork. Serve hot.

NOTE: This basic rice preparation is endlessly versatile: Use jasmine rice and serve it with any Asian-style main dish or stir-fry; use basmati and it can swing in an Indian direction; use regular long-grain rice and it'll be right at home alongside Southern California–style Mexican dishes like the fish tacos on page 166, or South American meat dishes like the grilled steak on page 140. Or substitute parsley for the cilantro and serve it with the grilled lamb chops on page 148.

Season 3, Episode 15

GLORIA:
If you have a problem with the way Manny's being raised, you talk to me!

JAY:
I am.

GLORIA:
I don't want to hear it!

MANNY:

So, is this the legendary rice pilaf we've been hearing about?

JAY:

Try it for yourself. I used to make it every year, but it, uh, started to upstage the turkey.

MANNY, AFTER TASTING A SPOONFUL:

Hmm.

JAY:

Something wrong?

MANNY:

Not so much wrong as missing. It just tastes a little flat.

JAY:

That a fact?

MANNY:

I just think with the earthiness of the rice, you might want something zesty to set it off. I think this might be a job for cumin.

jay's | rice pilaf

Serves 6

1½ cups basmati rice	1 teaspoon mustard seeds
4 tablespoons unsalted butter	½ cinnamon stick (2 inches long)
1 medium onion, minced	¼ cup dried currants
1 tablespoon cumin seeds	Kosher salt

1 Put the rice in a fine-mesh sieve and rinse with cold water until the water runs clear. Shake out the excess water and let drain for 5 minutes.

2 Meanwhile, melt the butter in a large saucepan. Add the onion and cook over medium-high heat until softened and lightly browned, about 5 minutes. Add the cumin and mustard seeds and the cinnamon stick and cook until fragrant, about 2 minutes. Add the rice and currants and stir to combine. Add 2½ cups water and a pinch of salt and bring to a boil, stirring. Cover and cook over low heat until the rice is tender and the water is absorbed, about 17 minutes. Fluff the rice with a fork, cover, and let sit for 5 minutes. Transfer to a bowl, remove the cinnamon stick, and serve right away.

jay's | broccoli *with* caramelized garlic *and* pine nuts

Serves 6

⅓ cup pine nuts

4 tablespoons unsalted butter

1 tablespoon olive oil

6 garlic cloves, thinly sliced

1 pound broccoli florets

½ teaspoon kosher salt

⅛ teaspoon crushed red pepper

1 Toast the pine nuts in a large skillet over medium heat for 6 minutes or until lightly browned. Remove from the skillet; set aside.

2 Heat the butter and oil in the same skillet over medium heat until the butter melts. Add the garlic and sauté for 1 to 2 minutes or until lightly browned. Add the broccoli, salt, and crushed red pepper; sauté for 8 minutes or until the broccoli is tender. Stir in the pine nuts and serve immediately.

NOTE: Be sure to watch the pine nuts closely, because they can blacken suddenly.

Season 5, Episode 11

GLORIA:
Jay, what do you like better—the accent or the balloons?

JAY:
I've been asking myself that since I met you.

GLORIA:
Ay!

ANDY:
Can I just say, I want this type of playful banter in my relationship.

JAY:
Long as you say it someplace else.

"I understand about twenty percent of what goes on around here."

— JAY

phil's | chunky cranberry applesauce

Makes about 3½ cups; serves 6 to 8

5 Gala apples, peeled and cubed

1 cup fresh or frozen cranberries

¼ cup sugar

1 teaspoon grated orange zest

1 Combine the apples, cranberries, and ½ cup water in a Dutch oven. Bring to a boil; cover, reduce the heat, and simmer, stirring occasionally, for 25 minutes or until the apples are tender.

2 Stir in the sugar and orange zest. Remove from the heat; mash the fruit mixture with a potato masher until chunky. Serve warm.

NOTE: This gorgeous pink, cranberry-studded applesauce, fragrant with orange zest, can be made several days in advance and reheated just before serving.

PHIL:

The cranberry sauce is okay, and the gravy is out of the woods.

LUKE:

And, thanks to you, those baby carrots are gonna pull through.

PHIL:

Well, they're fighters.

NIGELLA LAWSON'S VOICE (VIA HER COOKING APP):

And now, Philip, for the last time, lightly brush the thighs.

PHIL:

I'm gonna miss this randy little Redcoat. But it's time to cross the finish line.

claire's | green beans *with* toasted almonds *and* lemon

Serves 4

1 **tablespoon olive oil**	2 **tablespoons sliced almonds**
1 **pound green beans, trimmed**	1 **tablespoon fresh lemon juice**
1 **shallot, thinly sliced**	¼ **teaspoon kosher salt**
2 **teaspoons unsalted butter**	¼ **teaspoon freshly ground black pepper**

1 Heat a large skillet over medium heat. Add the oil; swirl to coat. Add the beans and shallot; cook for 5 minutes, stirring frequently. Add ½ cup water; cover and cook for 5 minutes or until the beans are crisp-tender.

2 Melt the butter in a small skillet over medium heat. Add the almonds; cook for 5 minutes or until browned, stirring frequently.

3 Add the almonds, lemon juice, salt, and pepper to bean mixture; toss well. Serve immediately.

KIDS CAN HELP!

With older kids who have practiced their cutting skills, let them trim the ends off the green beans with a child-safe knife. With the younger ones, teach them how to snap off the ends with their fingers.

Season 3, Episode 15

CLAIRE:
What was I thinking? I-I-I just get drunk, and I bring a baby into the world?

PHIL:
That would be four for four.

CLAIRE:
I can't go through with it.

PHIL:
Don't panic. You haven't donated anything yet. Besides, what are the chances your eggs even work? What are the chances we can pretend I never said that?

PHIL, FILMING CLAIRE:

Councilwoman Dunphy, how do you respond to allegations that you look super sexy in your new suit?

CLAIRE:

I haven't been elected yet ... Honey, come on, please stop filming.

PHIL:

I'm just excited. After today, you are going to be a councilwoman, and I am going to be a first husband.

CLAIRE:

Well, if you don't stop filming, you're going to be *my* first husband.

claire's | mashed potatoes

Serves 8

9 medium russet potatoes, cleaned and peeled

¾ cup milk

6 tablespoons unsalted butter or margarine

1 teaspoon kosher salt

Paprika (optional)

1 Cut the potatoes into quarters. Put the potatoes in a Dutch oven with enough water to cover them. Bring to a boil over high heat, then cover and cook over medium heat for 20 minutes or until tender.

2 Drain the potatoes and return them to the Dutch oven. Cook over low heat, stirring constantly, until the potatoes are dry. Remove from the heat; set aside.

3 Combine the milk and butter in a small saucepan. Cook over medium heat, stirring constantly, until the butter melts.

4 Mash the potatoes until smooth. Gradually add the milk mixture; stir well. Stir in the salt.

5 Transfer the potatoes to a serving bowl; sprinkle with paprika if you like. Serve warm.

VOTE

Claire Dunphy

for Town Council

HONESTY · INTEGRITY · TENACITY · MOTHER · NEIGHBOR · COUNCILWOMAN

The choice is Claire!

Here to hear your concerns. Making our town a safer place.

"If elected, I will do more than write one ordinance that allows private parties to have more than eight dogs."

★ For the people. ★

Claire **Dunphy**
The choice is Claire!
for **Town Council**

mr. tough guy

Whether she's fighting to make the neighborhood streets safer for her kids, or cursing at the manager of Scardino's for shortchanging her on her pizza, Claire Dunphy does not settle for mediocrity. Phil calls her "Mr. Tough Guy Problem-Solver" because the family turns to her whenever they need real results.

CLAIRE

VS

COUNCILMAN BAILEY

When Councilman Bailey continued to say no to the stop sign Claire wanted on her street, she decided to run against him for a city council seat. She lost the war, but she won the battle—the stop sign appeared shortly after the election.

THE NEIGHBORS

Claire's obnoxious, medical marijuana–selling neighbors are no match for her. She complained when they shot off fireworks. She complained about their drum set. She even hung up curtains so they couldn't peek in on her anymore.

THE PIZZA RESTAURANT

Claire would not back down when she was shortchanged by Scardino's—even though it meant being banned from the restaurant and forced to eat garbage pizza for the rest of her life.

THE SPEEDER

When an erratic driver began speeding past their house regularly, Claire and Luke not only shouted, "Slow down, jerk!" into a megaphone, they also posted signs all over the neighborhood declaring that it was time to "Slow down your neighbors."

DYLAN

Dylan's grand romantic gestures—his performance of "In the Moonlight (Do Me)," his proposal on the dude ranch, among others—may have endeared him to Haley and Phil, but Claire was never a fan.

HALEY

Claire not only rejected Dylan on Haley's behalf when he proposed, she also hacked Haley's Facebook account when Haley allegedly ran off to Vegas to marry Andy. Boundaries aren't really her thing, but the mom card usually gets her off the hook.

MITCHELL

Claire quit being Mitchell's ice-skating partner before the 13-and-under regional championships. Two decades later Mitchell was still upset that she denied him his chance at an Olympic gold medal.

MAIN COURSES

claire's | one-pot pasta *with* beans *and* spinach

Serves 4

- **6 ounces (about 1½ cups) uncooked gemelli (short tube-shaped pasta) or farfalle (bow-tie pasta)**
- **1 (15-ounce) can cannellini beans or other white beans**
- **4 cups torn spinach**
- **2 tablespoons extra-virgin olive oil**
- **2 tablespoons white balsamic vinegar**

- **1 tablespoon chopped fresh basil**
- **1 garlic clove, minced**
- **¼ teaspoon kosher salt**
- **½ cup (2 ounces) shredded Parmesan cheese**
- **½ teaspoon freshly ground black pepper**

1 Cook the pasta according to the package directions, omitting salt and fat.

2 Put the beans in a colander; pile the spinach on top of the beans. Set aside.

3 Combine the oil, vinegar, basil, garlic, and salt in a small bowl.

4 When the pasta is done, remove ¼ cup of the pasta water from the pan; stir it into the oil mixture. Pour the remaining pasta water and pasta over the spinach and beans in the colander.

5 Drain the pasta mixture well; place in a large serving bowl. Pour the oil mixture over the pasta mixture; toss well. Sprinkle with the cheese and pepper; toss well. Let stand for 5 minutes; serve warm.

Season 4, Episode 21

PHIL:
Okay, before you say no . . .

CLAIRE:
No.

PHIL:
You haven't even seen it yet.

CLAIRE:
Mm, I'm sticking with "No."

Season 2, Episode 19

CAM:

I was volunteering for [the] spring musical festival when their regular director suddenly and mysteriously became ill . . . It may have been a blessing. Their show lacked focus. I gave it a theme—"A Musical Trip Around the World."

MITCHELL:

Yeah, see, he focused it by making it about the world.

cam's | asparagus pita rounds

Serves 4

2 cups (2-inch) sliced asparagus (about 1 pound)

2 teaspoons extra-virgin olive oil

2 garlic cloves, minced

4 (6-inch) pitas

3 plum tomatoes, thinly sliced (about ½ pound)

1 teaspoon dried basil

¼ teaspoon crushed red pepper (optional)

¼ teaspoon kosher salt

6 tablespoons shredded Parmesan cheese

1 Preheat the oven to 450°F.

2 Steam the asparagus, covered, for 2 minutes or until crisp-tender; drain. Rinse with cold water; drain well.

3 Combine the oil and garlic; brush over the pitas. Arrange the tomato slices and asparagus on the pitas. Sprinkle with the basil, crushed red pepper, and salt. Top evenly with the cheese. Bake for 7 to 8 minutes or until the edges are golden. Serve immediately.

cam *the* renaissance man

Not many people can do it all, but Cam Tucker sure can.
He's a husband. He's a dad. He's an artist, a musician, a photographer, a cowboy,
a football coach, a workingman — and he's got an outfit for every occasion.

- **Cowboy Cam**
  Being a rancher runs in Cam's blood, but he's more than just boots and belt buckles. He can rope and ride and shoot with the best of them. (And once he's back home, he can put together a glitter-filled scrapbook to commemorate his time on the range.)

- **Clown Cam**
  Whether it's a family birthday party, a funeral, a lesson in laughs for Lily "Lizbo" Tucker-Pritchett, or just a way to deal with anxiety (he sleep-clowns), Cam is always ready to don his purple wig, his red nose, and his too-big shoes.

- **Lily-Wranglin' Cam**
  From lassoing Lily with a "child safety tether" on a family vacation to scooping her up and dragging her away from the all-white couch at home, Cam is great at keeping Lily out of trouble (and away from the designer furniture).

- **Workingman Cam**
  Anything a straight man can do, Cam can do better. Build a princess castle? Check. Drive a moving truck? Check. Destroy the strongman hammer game at the fall festival? Check. Fashion a mermaid costume for the cat? Check.

- **Substitute Teacher Cam**
  Cam can bring the treble to Luke's music class and the American Revolution to Alex's AP history class, and he can do it all in character.

- **Musical Cam**
  Cam has starred in several local theater troupe productions, but his musical prowess doesn't end there. He's also been a drummer in Dylan's band, a high school music teacher, and Lily's personal voice coach.

- **Punkin Chunkin Champion Cam**
  It hurts Cam's feelings when Claire thinks he's lying about having won the Punkin Chunkin championship in his hometown, but she's proven wrong when she watches him launch a pumpkin so far—the length of a football field!—that it dents the side of his car.

- **Football Coach Cam**
  Cam was born to be a football coach. He knows how to recruit, how to design plays, and how to inspire his team. Most of all, he knows how to celebrate a hard-earned victory with grace and good sports-manship. ("I won! I won! I mean, we won! We won! We won!")

- **Party Planner Cam**
  He's got an eye for design, an ear for music, a taste for hors d'oeuvres, and complete devotion to party themes. He even owns his own headsets! And when the party seems like it might flop, Cam's not afraid to send out unvitations, or consider burning down his own house.

- **Husband Cam**
  "In this relationship, I'm the gas pedal and you're the brakes," Cam tells Mitchell. He believes Mitchell has it in him to be a Supreme Court justice one day (and not just because he wants to say his husband is one of the Supremes at parties). He can even understand Mitchell when he's talking with a mouth full of toothpaste.

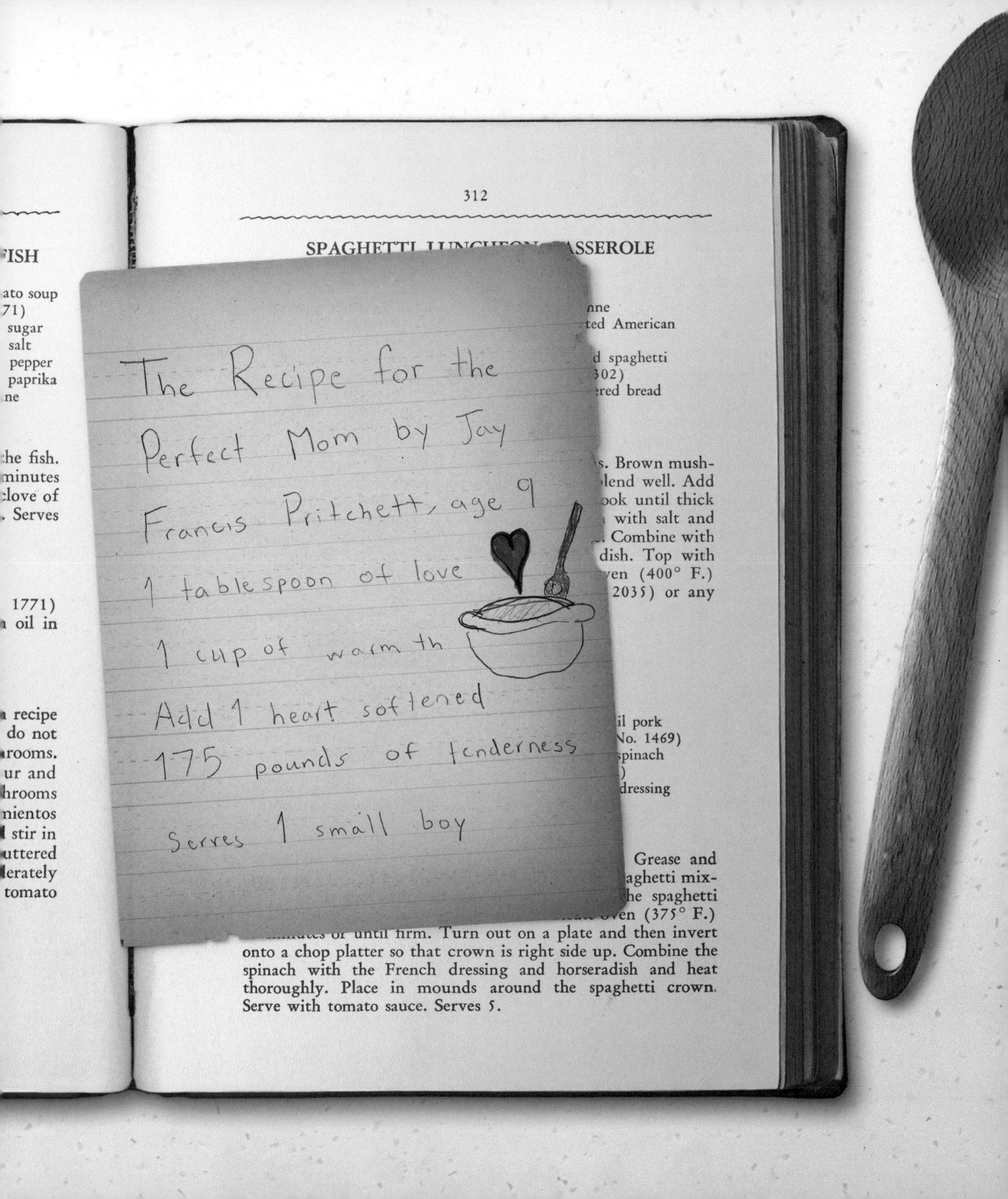

SPAGHETTI LUNCHEON CASSEROLE

FISH

ato soup
71)
sugar
salt
pepper
paprika
ne

the fish.
minutes
clove of
. Serves

1771)
oil in

a recipe
do not
rooms.
ur and
hrooms
nientos
stir in
uttered
erately
tomato

nne
ed American
d spaghetti
302)
ered bread

s. Brown mush-
lend well. Add
ook until thick
with salt and
. Combine with
dish. Top with
ven (400° F.)
2035) or any

l pork
No. 1469)
spinach
)
dressing

The Recipe for the

Perfect Mom by Jay

Francis Pritchett, age 9

1 tablespoon of love

1 cup of warmth

Add 1 heart softened

175 pounds of tenderness

Serves 1 small boy

Grease and
aghetti mix-
he spaghetti
oven (375° F.)
minutes or until firm. Turn out on a plate and then invert
onto a chop platter so that crown is right side up. Combine the
spinach with the French dressing and horseradish and heat
thoroughly. Place in mounds around the spaghetti crown.
Serve with tomato sauce. Serves 5.

jay's | mother's tomato sauce *with* spaghetti

Serves 4 to 6

¼ cup extra-virgin olive oil

1 small onion, finely chopped

2 garlic cloves, minced

1 tablespoon tomato paste

1 (35-ounce) can whole peeled Italian tomatoes, coarsely pureed in a blender

Kosher salt and freshly ground black pepper

½ teaspoon dried oregano, crumbled

Pinch of sugar

2 fresh basil sprigs

1 pound dried spaghetti

Freshly grated Parmesan cheese

1 In a large saucepan, heat the oil. Add the onion and garlic and cook over medium heat, stirring occasionally, until golden, about 5 minutes. Add the tomato paste and cook, stirring constantly, for 1 minute or until brick-colored. Add the tomatoes and season with salt and pepper. Stir in the oregano, sugar, and basil and bring to a boil. Simmer, uncovered, over low heat, stirring occasionally, until thickened and reduced to 3 cups, about 30 minutes. Discard the basil sprigs. (The sauce can be cooled and then refrigerated for up to 3 days or frozen for up to 1 month.)

2 Cook the spaghetti in a very large pot of salted water until al dente. Drain the pasta and return it to the pot. Add half of the marinara sauce and cook over medium heat for 1 minute, tossing. Transfer to a serving bowl and top with the remaining sauce. Pass the cheese on the side.

Season 2, Episode 21

JAY, AFTER SEEING PHIL'S GOGGLES:
What the hell are those?

PHIL:
Onion goggles. No more tears when I cook. Welcome to the twenty-first century. You should get a pair.

JAY:
I was gonna suggest the same thing.

PHIL:
Here, Jay, you know what we should put in this? We should add a dash—

JAY:
No! It's my mom's recipe. Whatever it says on the page goes in the pot. Nothing more, nothing less.

Season 5, Episode 6

ANDY:

Hi. I'm Andy. I'm [Joan's] manny—male nanny.

GLORIA:

Hi. I'm Gloria. This might just sound a little crazy, but I don't think Joan likes me.

ANDY:

Oh, that's not crazy. She doesn't. Her husband's always staring at you, and she's worried you're gonna steal him.

GLORIA:

What?!... I would never steal anybody else's man, especially not her fat husband.

ANDY:

Hey, he's not fat anymore. I helped him lose thirty pounds.

andy's | partly egg-white mediterranean-style frittata

Serves 4

2 teaspoons olive oil

¾ cup packed baby spinach

2 green onions

4 large egg whites

6 large eggs

⅓ cup (about 1½ ounces) crumbled feta cheese with basil and sun-dried tomatoes

2 teaspoons salt-free Greek seasoning (such as Cavender's)

¼ teaspoon kosher salt

1 Preheat the broiler.

2 Heat the oil in a 10-inch ovenproof skillet over medium heat. While the oil heats, coarsely chop the spinach and finely chop the green onions. Combine the egg whites, whole eggs, cheese, Greek seasoning, and salt in a large bowl; stir well with a whisk. Add the spinach and onions, stirring well.

3 Add the egg mixture to the pan; cook until the edges begin to set, about 2 minutes. Gently lift the edge of the egg mixture, tilting the pan to allow uncooked egg mixture to come in contact with the pan. Cook for 2 minutes or until the egg mixture is almost set.

4 Broil for 2 to 3 minutes or until the center is set. Transfer the frittata to a serving platter immediately; cut into 4 wedges and serve.

sloppy jay's

Serves 8

3 pounds ground beef, browned and drained

1 onion, finely chopped

1 green bell pepper, chopped

1 (28-ounce) can tomato sauce

¾ cup ketchup

3 tablespoons Worcestershire sauce

1 teaspoon chili powder

½ teaspoon freshly ground black pepper

½ teaspoon garlic powder

8 sandwich buns, split

1 Combine all the ingredients except the buns in a 5-quart slow cooker. Cover and cook on the low setting for 4 hours. Serve on the buns.

Season 1, Episode 8

JAY:

All the grandkids are coming over for "Jay's Night." Family tradition. Everybody wears PJs—which they love. I make my famous Sloppy Jay's—which are Sloppy Joe's, but made by Jay—which they love. And then we all watch a Western together—which they don't really care for, but, hey, it's "Jay's Night."

Season 2, Episode 22

JAY:

You've got to learn to say no to people.

GLORIA:

Fine. Ask me if you can go golfing now.

JAY:

Other people.

GLORIA:

All I want is when I go to bed at night to be laying next to a man that is generous and giving. And that man doesn't necessarily need to be you.

jay's | grilled beef tenderloin *with* chimichurri

Serves 4

2 **garlic cloves**

1 **teaspoon sugar**

½ **teaspoon kosher salt**

4 **(4-ounce) beef tenderloin steaks, trimmed**

Cooking spray

½ **cup Smoky Chimichurri (recipe follows)**

1 Preheat a grill, hibachi, grill pan, or wood-fired device to medium-high heat. To test this, hover your hand, palm side down, about 4 inches above the grate and count how long you can hold it there comfortably. Three to four seconds is the sign it's reached medium-high heat (350 to 400°F).

2 Peel the garlic cloves. Snip the woody ends off the cloves. Place the garlic cloves on a cutting board (preferably wooden) and pour the sugar and salt over the cloves. Roughly chop the garlic-sugar-salt mixture until pieces are about the size of grains of rice. Then, using the side of your knife, pull the blade across the chopped mixture to mash it to a paste. Repeat the process until there is a uniform paste. Rub the paste evenly on both sides of the steaks.

3 Grill on a grill rack coated with cooking spray for about 2½ minutes on each side for medium-rare, 4 minutes on each side (no more than 8 minutes total) for medium. Place the finished steaks on a plate and allow them to rest for 10 minutes before "flashing" them on the grill or grill pan—cooking them briefly to reheat the surfaces. Serve with the chimichurri.

NOTE: If you want to make Jay proud, pull these beautiful steaks off the grill just before you think they're ready.

smoky chimichurri

Makes about ½ cup; serves 4

½ cup fresh flat-leaf parsley, coarsely chopped

3 tablespoons minced shallot

2 garlic cloves, minced

1 teaspoon dried oregano

¼ teaspoon kosher salt

⅛ teaspoon crushed red pepper

⅛ teaspoon freshly ground black pepper

⅛ teaspoon smoked paprika

1 tablespoon extra-virgin olive oil

3 tablespoons sherry vinegar

1 teaspoon fresh lemon juice

1 Combine all but the liquid ingredients in a mortar and pestle or a durable mixing bowl (you can use the blunt end of a rolling pin if you don't have a mortar and pestle). Pound the mixture firmly. When the mixture looks shaggy and the juices of the shallot seem to have moistened the mass, stir in the oil, continually pounding and vigorously mixing for another minute. Let rest for 10 minutes or so to weep and wilt further.

2 Stir in the vinegar and the lemon juice using a spoon. Either in the refrigerator or at room temperature, let rest for about 30 minutes before serving to spoon over grilled meats.

"A thousand therapists couldn't do what Gloria did for me."

— JAY

gloria's | grilled steak wraps *with* avocado pico de gallo

Serves 6

8 ounces flank steak

1 tablespoon salt-free fajita or Mexican seasoning

2 medium poblano peppers, halved and seeded

1 red bell pepper, halved and seeded

1 yellow bell pepper, halved and seeded

3 tablespoons fresh lime juice

2 tablespoons chopped fresh cilantro

3 teaspoons olive oil

½ teaspoon freshly ground black pepper

Avocado Pico de Gallo (recipe follows)

Cooking spray

1 large onion, sliced

6 (10-inch) flour tortillas

6 tablespoons sour cream

¾ cup shredded Cheddar cheese

1 Rub both sides of the meat with the fajita seasoning; place in a large zip-top plastic bag and marinate in the refrigerator for at least 8 hours and up to overnight.

2 Put the poblano and bell peppers in a zip-top plastic bag. Stir together the lime juice, cilantro, 2 teaspoons of the oil, and the black pepper; pour over the peppers and seal the bag. Marinate in the refrigerator for at least 2 hours and up to overnight.

3 Prepare the pico de gallo; cover and chill in the refrigerator.

4 Prepare an outdoor grill for direct cooking over medium-high heat.

5 Place the meat and peppers (skin sides down) on the grill grate coated with cooking spray; grill, covered, for 12 minutes. Remove the peppers and put them in a zip-top plastic bag to steam for 10 minutes. Turn the meat and grill for an additional 10 minutes or until desired degree of doneness. Let stand for 5 minutes. Cut the meat diagonally across the grain into thin slices. Remove the skins from the peppers and cut them into strips.

continued on next page

Season 6, Episode 22

JAY:

Gloria's about to take her citizenship test. This little jumping bean is about to become an American.

GLORIA:

Jumping beans are Mexican.

JAY:

Once you're an American you won't see the difference.

6 Heat the remaining 1 teaspoon oil in a large nonstick skillet over medium heat. Add the onion; sauté for 15 minutes or until lightly browned.

7 Heat the tortillas according to the package directions.

8 Divide the meat and vegetables evenly among the tortillas. Top each tortilla with 1 tablespoon sour cream, 2½ tablespoons pico de gallo, and 2 tablespoons cheese; roll up.

NOTE: Flank steak is great cooked low and slow in a braised dish, but when grilled, it's best cooked hot and fast.

avocado pico de gallo

Makes 1 cup

½ cup finely chopped ripe avocado

½ cup finely chopped plum tomato

2 tablespoons finely chopped green onions

1 tablespoon fresh lime juice

¼ teaspoon kosher salt

⅛ teaspoon freshly ground black pepper

2 garlic cloves, pressed

1 Stir all the ingredients together in a small bowl. Mix well. Cover and chill in the refrigerator.

phil's | lamb sandwich

Serves 4

2 teaspoons ground cumin

½ teaspoon dried oregano

2 garlic cloves, minced

3 tablespoons fresh lemon juice

¼ cup extra-virgin olive oil

Kosher salt

1 pound lamb shoulder, lightly trimmed and very thinly sliced

1 large white onion, cut into thin slivers

¼ cup tahini (sesame paste)

½ cup Greek-style full-fat yogurt

Hot sauce, chopped lettuce, sliced tomatoes, rice, and warmed pita for serving

1 In a large bowl, combine the cumin and oregano with half of the garlic and 1 tablespoon of the lemon juice. Add the oil and a generous pinch of salt. Add the lamb and onion and let sit at room temperature for 30 minutes.

2 Meanwhile, in a blender or mini chopper, combine the tahini with ½ cup water, the remaining garlic, and the remaining 2 tablespoons lemon juice and puree until smooth. Add the yogurt and process until creamy. Season with salt. The sauce can be refrigerated for up to 4 days.

3 Heat a large griddle or two skillets until very hot. Add the lamb and onion and cook over high heat, turning occasionally, until charred and tender, 6 to 7 minutes. Serve the lamb with the tahini sauce, hot sauce, lettuce, tomatoes, rice, and warmed pita.

Season 5, Episode 5

PHIL:
Well, do you like this suit? I wouldn't know because all you said was, "It's tight," and not in a cool black way.

CLAIRE:
Wait, a-are you trying to say that you squeezed yourself in that for me?

THE MAGICAL MADNESS OF
phil dunphy's brain

Phil is constantly trying to find a balance between being a fun dad, a supportive husband, a beloved son-in-law, a successful real estate agent, and an all-around cool guy. It probably looks a little bit like this inside his mixed-up noggin.

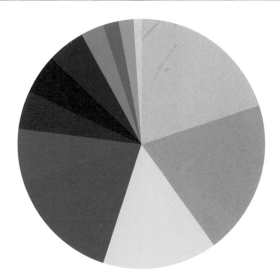

- **20% Skip Woosnum**
"Oooh, here's something that jumps right off the page. I tried this yesterday, thanks to my good friend Skip Woosnum. Claire, do your-self a favor and join me in a wedge salad."

- **20% Mnemonic devices**
"Um, like the other day, I met this guy Carl and I might forget that name, but he was wearing a Grateful Dead T-shirt. What's a band like the Grateful Dead? Phish. Where do fish live? The ocean. What else is in the ocean? Coral. Hello, Carl."

- **15% Claire**
"Sometimes I don't know if I love how much I fear Claire or fear how much I love her."

- **15% Peer-enting**
"I've always said that if my son thinks of me as one of his idiot friends, I've succeeded as a dad."

- **7% Winning over Jay**
"I've been practicing like crazy. All my cowboy skills. Shootin', ropin', pancake eatin'. Why? Because sometimes I feel like Jay doesn't respect me as a man."

- **5% Magic**
"It goes without saying that the butler's escape is one of the most challenging feats of escap-ology an illusionist can perform."

- **5% Cheerleading**
"Cheerleading in my college was cool. The football players were so jealous they wouldn't even let me and my buddies, Trevor, Scotty, and Ling, go to their parties."

- **5% Inventions**
"We are about to make hat history. Or, as I like to call it, hatstory."

- **3% Apple products**
"The iPad comes out. On my actual birthday. It's like Steve Jobs and God got together to say, 'We love you, Phil.'"

- **2% Real estate**
"You can insult a lot of things about me—my hair, my voice, my balance-board exercises—but don't insult my selling. That crosses a line. What line? Oh, you don't see it? That's because I just sold it!"

- **2% Scary clowns**
"I am not really sure where the fear comes from. My mother says it's because when I was a kid, I found a dead clown in the woods, but who knows?"

- **1% That broken step**
"Gotta fix that step!"

phil's | lamb chops *with* minted yogurt

Serves 4

½ cup plain yogurt (regular or Greek)

1 tablespoon chopped fresh mint

1 teaspoon fresh lemon juice

1 small garlic clove, minced

½ teaspoon kosher salt

½ teaspoon freshly ground black pepper

8 (4-ounce) lamb loin chops, trimmed

Cooking spray

1 Prepare an outdoor grill for cooking over medium-high heat.

2 Combine the yogurt, mint, lemon juice, and garlic. Stir in ⅛ teaspoon of the salt and ⅛ teaspoon of the pepper. Chill in the refrigerator.

3 Sprinkle the lamb evenly with the remaining ⅜ teaspoon each salt and pepper. Place the lamb on the grill rack coated with cooking spray; grill for 3 minutes on each side or until desired degree of doneness. Serve with the yogurt sauce.

TIP: Try these with the cilantro rice on page 116, or the quinoa salad on page 89.

CLAIRE, REFERRING TO PHIL'S STREETSTRIDER:

Honey, you finally found something less cool than those pants that zip off into shorts.

PHIL:

My shants, which you have been gunning for since day one.

CLAIRE:

Mm-hmm.

PHIL:

Does it matter to any of you that this is actually an extremely efficient cardiovascular workout that could prolong my life?

CLAIRE:

Mm, yeah. But what kind of life? And with whom?

the *dunphys'* | meat loaf *with* quick gravy

Season 4, Episode 3

CLAIRE:

I will deal with it tomorrow, but today I'm taking your father to the doctor.

LUKE:

He's having an ass-ectomy.

PHIL:

What?

LUKE:

I hear things.

HALEY:

You're getting your tonsils out?

ALEX:

Oh, this family needs a dumbass-ectomy.

Serves 4

½ cup finely chopped onion

½ cup finely chopped green bell pepper

½ cup uncooked rolled oats

1 teaspoon dried oregano

2 teaspoons Worcestershire sauce

¼ teaspoon kosher salt

¼ teaspoon freshly ground black pepper

2 large egg whites

1 pound ground round

Cooking spray

Quick Gravy (recipe follows)

2 tablespoons chopped fresh parsley (optional)

1 Preheat the oven to 350°F.

2 Combine the onion, bell pepper, oats, oregano, Worcestershire sauce, salt, black pepper, and egg whites in a large bowl; crumble the beef over the vegetable mixture and stir until well blended. Shape the beef mixture into an 8-by-4-inch loaf. Place a rack in a shallow baking pan and spray them with cooking spray. Place the meat loaf on the rack. Bake until a thermometer inserted into the center registers 160°F, about 55 minutes.

3 Prepare the gravy.

4 Remove the meat loaf from the oven. Let stand for 10 minutes. Cut into slices. Serve with gravy, sprinkled with parsley, if desired.

NOTE: Meat loaf is quite adaptable. If you don't have a bell pepper, use minced or grated carrots instead, or a half-block of thawed and squeezed-out frozen spinach; use dry bread crumbs instead of oats; double the recipe and make two loaves for heartier appetites.

quick gravy

Makes about 1⅓ cups

3 tablespoons all-purpose flour

1 (14½-ounce) can beef broth

⅛ teaspoon freshly ground black pepper

¼ cup evaporated milk

1 tablespoon unsalted butter or margarine

1 Place a large nonstick skillet over medium-high heat until hot. Add the flour and cook for 6 to 8 minutes or until golden, stirring constantly.

2 Whisk in the broth and pepper. Cook for 8 to 10 minutes or until thickened, stirring often. Stir in the evaporated milk; cook for 2 minutes. Remove from the heat; stir in the butter. Serve hot.

DEAN MILLER:

Miss Dunphy, is there anything you would like to say in your defense?

HALEY:

Actually, I have no defense. I was drinking. I am underage. I ran from the police, and even though it was an accident, I injured an officer. I am very, very sorry. I've made a lot of bad decisions since I've been here, and it's time I take some responsibility. Like sometimes, in the dining hall, I slip my pinkie under the scale when they weigh my salad. Also, I've missed more morning classes than I've been to.

CLAIRE:

She's kidding.

HALEY:

I don't know what the policy is on dating TAs, but I think I broke it. . . . Twice.

haley's | ramen pizza hack

Serves 2

1 package instant ramen, seasoning packet discarded

½ cup prepared tomato sauce

½ cup shredded mozzarella

10 slices pepperoni

1 Preheat the oven to 450°F.

2 Top the ramen with the tomato sauce, cheese, and pepperoni and bake directly on the rack until the cheese is melted, about 8 minutes.

jay's | barbecued pork shoulder

Serves 8 to 10

1 medium onion, minced

1 garlic clove, minced

½ cup (1 stick) unsalted butter or margarine, melted

1 cup ketchup

½ cup cider vinegar

1 cup firmly packed brown sugar

Zest of 1 lemon, chopped

1½ tablespoons fresh lemon juice

2 tablespoons Worcestershire sauce

1 teaspoon hot sauce

½ teaspoon chili powder

1 (6- to 7-pound) pork shoulder roast

1 In a small saucepan, sauté the onion and garlic in the butter over medium heat until tender. Add the ketchup, vinegar, ½ cup water, the brown sugar, lemon zest and juice, Worcestershire sauce, hot sauce, and chili powder; cook until hot. Set the barbecue sauce aside.

2 Prepare a grill for cooking indirectly over low heat. Place the pork shoulder on the grill grate. Cover the grill; open the vent. Grill for 3 hours, turning occasionally. Baste the pork with the barbecue sauce. Continue to grill for 1 hour or until the pork is tender, basting frequently with the sauce. Remove to a baking dish and shred the pork with two forks. Stir in a little more sauce, if desired, and serve.

TIP: Serve the shredded meat on soft buns or plain, with a few potluck-style sides.

Season 1, Episode 24

JAY:

Where's my good underwear?

GLORIA:

The question is, why isn't all your underwear good, Jay? You make a nice living.

jay's | fresh tomato, sausage, *and* pecorino pasta

Serves 8 to 10

8 ounces dried penne pasta

8 ounces sweet Italian sausage

2 teaspoons olive oil

1 cup sliced onion

2 teaspoons minced garlic

1¼ pounds tomatoes, chopped

6 tablespoons grated pecorino Romano cheese

¼ teaspoon salt

⅛ teaspoon freshly ground black pepper

¼ cup torn fresh basil leaves

1 Cook the pasta according to the package directions, omitting salt and fat. Drain and keep warm.

2 Heat a large nonstick skillet over medium-high heat. Remove the casings from the sausage. Add the oil to the pan and swirl to coat. Add the sausage and onion; cook for 4 minutes, stirring to crumble the sausage. Add the garlic; cook for 2 minutes. Stir in the tomatoes; cook for 2 minutes. Remove from the heat and stir in the pasta, 2 tablespoons of the cheese, the salt, and the pepper. Sprinkle with the remaining 4 tablespoons cheese and the basil and serve immediately.

Season 2, Episiode 24

JAY:

Sausage of the Month Club really nailed it in May. But, honey, no offense, they almost lost me last month with that chorizo.

GLORIA:

Why no offense? It's a sausage, it's not on our flag.

"I know that I have an accent, but people understand me just fine!"

— GLORIA —

gloria's | pernil asado

Serves 8 to 10

- **1 head garlic, peeled and smashed**
- **2 tablespoons ground cumin**
- **1 tablespoon achiote powder**
- **1 tablespoon kosher salt**
- **1 tablespoon freshly ground black pepper**
- **2 tablespoons fresh lime juice**
- **1 (6- to 7-pound) bone-in pork shoulder with skin**
- **2 (12-ounce) bottles lager**

1 In a mini chopper, combine the garlic, cumin, achiote, salt, pepper, and lime juice and blend until smooth. Using a small, sharp paring knife, deeply poke the pork all over. Rub the pork with the spice mixture, pressing it into the gashes. Refrigerate overnight.

2 Put the pork shoulder in a roasting pan and add the beer. Let sit at room temperature for 1 hour, turning once or twice.

3 Preheat the oven to 275°F.

4 Roast the pork, covered with foil, for 4 hours, then remove the foil and roast until an instant-read thermometer registers 180°F, 2 to 3 hours longer, adding water if the pan becomes too dry. Cover loosely with the foil if the skin darkens too quickly. Let rest for 30 minutes, then remove the skin and cut the meat into thick slices. Cut the crisp skin into pieces and serve on the side.

TIP: Serve with plenty of fluffy rice, some basic black beans, and a fresh tomato salad like the one on page 91.

NOTE: Look for the deep brick-red ground achiote seeds in Latin American grocery stores—the package might be labeled "annatto."

Season 2, Episode 6

JAY:
Listen, did you ever do anything about costumes for Claire's thing tonight?

GLORIA:
I'm going to pick them up this afternoon. You're going to be a gargle, and I'm gonna be an evil village bruja.

JAY:
I know less now than I did before I asked.

GLORIA:
A bruja is a witch, and a gargle is a gargle.

MANNY:
She means gargoyle.

GLORIA:
That's what I said.

gloria-english dictionary

Gloria's accent is a big part of her charm, but it can occasionally lead to some confusion on the receiving end. Use this handy guide to break down the pronunciation barrier and translate her frequent malapropisms.

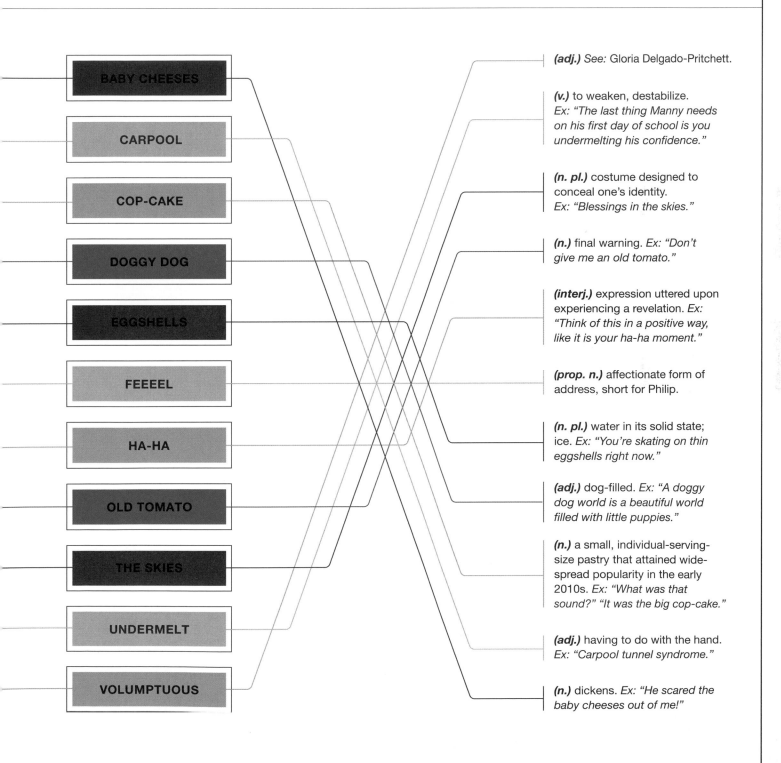

BABY CHEESES

CARPOOL

COP-CAKE

DOGGY DOG

EGGSHELLS

FEEEEL

HA-HA

OLD TOMATO

THE SKIES

UNDERMELT

VOLUMPTUOUS

(adj.) See: Gloria Delgado-Pritchett.

(v.) to weaken, destabilize. *Ex: "The last thing Manny needs on his first day of school is you undermelting his confidence."*

(n. pl.) costume designed to conceal one's identity. *Ex: "Blessings in the skies."*

(n.) final warning. *Ex: "Don't give me an old tomato."*

(interj.) expression uttered upon experiencing a revelation. *Ex: "Think of this in a positive way, like it is your ha-ha moment."*

(prop. n.) affectionate form of address, short for Philip.

(n. pl.) water in its solid state; ice. *Ex: "You're skating on thin eggshells right now."*

(adj.) dog-filled. *Ex: "A doggy dog world is a beautiful world filled with little puppies."*

(n.) a small, individual-serving-size pastry that attained widespread popularity in the early 2010s. *Ex: "What was that sound?" "It was the big cop-cake."*

(adj.) having to do with the hand. *Ex: "Carpool tunnel syndrome."*

(n.) dickens. *Ex: "He scared the baby cheeses out of me!"*

gloria's | carnitas al diablo

Serves 4 to 6

- 2 **tablespoons tomato paste**
- 2 **tablespoons adobo sauce (from a can of chipotle chilies)**
- 3 **tablespoons chopped garlic**
- 1 **tablespoon chili powder**
- 1 **teaspoon kosher salt**
- 1 **teaspoon freshly ground black pepper**
- 3 **pounds boneless Boston butt pork roast, cut into 2-inch pieces**
- 1 **cup beer or low-sodium chicken broth**

1 Combine the tomato paste, adobo, garlic, chili powder, salt, and pepper in a 5- to 6-quart slow cooker; stir in the pork. Microwave the beer in a 2-cup glass measuring cup on high power for 2 minutes or until very hot. Pour the beer over the meat in the slow cooker; do not stir. Cover and cook on the high setting for 6 hours or until very tender.

2 Shred the meat using two forks. Serve hot, or see the note below.

NOTE: If you decide to make the meat ahead of time, transfer the meat and juices to a 13-by-9-inch baking dish; cover and refrigerate overnight. To reheat, crumble the meat mixture into a large skillet and cook over medium-high heat for 15 minutes or until browned and hot. If you prefer to use a microwave for reheating, microwave 6 cups of the meat mixture on high power, stirring once, for 6 minutes or until thoroughly heated through.

TIP: Serve in corn tortillas with onion, cilantro, avocado, lime wedges, and radishes on the side. If your tolerance for heat runs more toward Gloria's end of the spectrum than Cam's, increase the chili powder and adobo.

Season 1, Episode 18

GLORIA:
Are you okay?

CAM, SWEATING:
I'm fine.

GLORIA:
Are you sure?

CAM:
I love this place!

GLORIA:
But your head is running water.

CAM:
Oh, I don't think it is.

GLORIA:
I told you it was too spicy for you. Look at your shirt!

Season 3, Episode 5

MANNY:

It's the "Bieber-ization" of America.

JAY:

What do beavers have to do with anything?

GLORIA:

The beavers, they build the dams all over the country, so there's no floods. It's the beaverization of the Americas.

MANNY:

I'm finding there's less and less we can talk about.

gloria's | pork estofado *with* yucca

Serves 6

2 tablespoons ground cumin

1 teaspoon dried oregano, crumbled

2 teaspoons achiote powder (see Note on page 157)

½ cup canola or olive oil

3½ pounds boneless pork shoulder, cut into 1½-inch pieces

Kosher salt and freshly ground black pepper

1 large Spanish onion, cut into thick slivers

4 garlic cloves, smashed

1 (15-ounce) can diced tomatoes

4 cups chicken broth

4 large carrots, cut into 1-inch pieces

1 pound yucca, peeled and cut into 1½-inch chunks

White rice, sliced scallions, chopped avocado, and fresh cilantro leaves for serving

1 In a large bowl, combine the cumin, oregano, achiote, and ¼ cup of the oil. Add the pork and season with salt and pepper. Add the onion and garlic, turning and moving to coat all the pieces. Cover and refrigerate overnight.

2 In a large enameled cast-iron casserole with a lid or a Dutch oven, heat the remaining ¼ cup oil. Pick out the onion and garlic from the bowl. Working in batches, cook the pork over medium-high heat until brown and crusty all over, 8 to 10 minutes per batch. Transfer to a plate. Add the onion and garlic to the casserole and cook over medium heat until barely softened, about 5 minutes. Return the pork to the casserole and add the tomatoes and broth. Bring to a boil, cover, and simmer over low heat, stirring occasionally, until the pork is nearly tender, about 1½ hours.

3 Add the carrots and yucca, cover, and cook over low heat until the vegetables are tender but not mushy and the pork is fork-tender, about 30 minutes longer.

4 Serve over white rice and garnish with scallions, avocado, and cilantro.

cam's | pork pho

Serves 4 to 6

8 ounces flat rice stick noodles (bánh pho)

1 pound pork tenderloin, trimmed

3 teaspoons dark sesame oil

⅛ teaspoon ground red pepper

2 garlic cloves, minced

1 (1-inch) piece peeled fresh ginger, thinly sliced

½ medium onion, sliced

4 cups low-sodium beef broth

2 whole star anise

1 (3-inch) cinnamon stick

1½ tablespoons fish sauce

1 small red Thai chili, seeded

1¼ cups fresh bean sprouts

½ cup fresh basil leaves, coarsely chopped

10 lime wedges

1 Put the noodles in a large bowl. Add boiling water to cover; let stand for 20 minutes. Drain.

2 While the noodles are soaking, cut the tenderloin in half lengthwise. Cut each strip crosswise into thin slices. Heat 2 teaspoons of the sesame oil in a Dutch oven over medium-high heat. Add the pork, red pepper, and garlic; sauté for 3 to 4 minutes on each side or until the pork is lightly browned. Remove the pork mixture from the pot and set aside.

3 Heat the remaining 1 teaspoon sesame oil in the pot over medium-high heat. Add the ginger and onion; sauté for 3 minutes or until the onion is tender. Add the broth, 2 cups water, the star anise, cinnamon stick, fish sauce, and chili; bring to a boil. Reduce the heat and simmer, uncovered, for 15 minutes or until the liquid is reduced by one-third, to about 3¾ cups. Strain the broth through a metal sieve into a large bowl; discard the solids. Keep the broth warm.

4 Divide the bean sprouts among serving bowls; top with the noodles. Arrange the pork evenly over the noodles. Ladle the broth over the pork; top with the basil. Squeeze 1 lime wedge over each serving. Serve immediately with the remaining lime wedges.

Season 4, Episode 19

MITCHELL, TASTING HIS SOUP:
Mmm! So good.

CAM:
Mmm! Mmm!

LILY:
I want a cheeseburger.

CAM:
But this is a special soup called pho.

LILY:
You told me not to say that word.

GLORIA:
It is delicious. This is the food of your people.

BILLINGSLEY ACADEMY

PRESCHOOL – APPLICATION FOR ENROLLMENT

Due December 1, 2010

Birthdate: 03/02/08 Sex: M (F)
MM/DD/YY

Date: 10/23/10

Name: Lily _____ Tucker-Pritchett
FIRST   MIDDLE   LAST

Home Address: 276 Cresthill Avenue   State: CA   Zip Code: 91302

City: Oak Park

Parent/Guardian's Name: Cameron Tucker   Occupation: Renaissance Man

Parent/Guardian's Name: Mitchell Pritchett   Occupation: Environmental Lawyer

State important factors that Billingsley should know about your child (health, social, emotional).

Adopted from Vietnam, raised in a loving home by two same-sex life partners
(one parent is 1/8) (one parent is 1/16 Cherokee)

Please describe your child's personality.

Easygoing, expressive, definitely not a biter!

What kinds of activities does s/he especially enjoy?

Finger painting, photo shoots, shopping, playing with duckies

How did you hear about Billingsley Academy?

From its reputation as the Harvard of preschools

CONT.

1

the tucker-pritchetts' | bánh mì

Serves 4

FOR THE PICKLES:

½ cup rice vinegar

⅓ cup sugar

2 teaspoons sambal oelek

½ cup grated carrot

⅓ cup matchstick-cut radishes

⅓ cup thinly sliced red onion

FOR THE SANDWICHES:

6 (2-ounce) boneless pork
breakfast cutlets

¼ teaspoon kosher salt

Cooking spray

1 (12-ounce) French baguette
(16 inches long)

¼ cup light mayonnaise

1 teaspoon sambal oelek

¼ cup thinly sliced peeled
cucumber

½ cup fresh cilantro leaves

1 Make the pickles: Combine the vinegar, sugar, ⅓ cup water, and the sambal oelek in a small saucepan. Bring to a boil, stirring until the sugar dissolves. Remove from the heat. Add the carrot, radishes, and onion. Let stand, uncovered, at room temperature for 1 hour.

2 Make the sandwiches: Preheat the broiler.

3 Place the pork between two sheets of plastic wrap; pound to ⅛-inch thickness using a meat mallet or small heavy skillet. Unwrap the pork and sprinkle evenly with the salt; place on a broiler pan coated with cooking spray. Broil for 5 minutes. Remove from the pan.

4 Cut the bread in half lengthwise. Hollow out the bottom half of the bread, leaving a ½-inch-thick shell; reserve the torn bread for another use. Place the bread halves, cut sides up, on a baking sheet. Broil for 1 minute or until toasted.

5 Combine the mayonnaise and sambal oelek in a small bowl; spread on the cut side of the bread top. Layer the pickled vegetables, pork slices, cucumber, and cilantro evenly on the bread bottom. Cover with the bread top. Cut the sandwich into 4 equal portions and serve immediately.

Season 3, Episode 21

MITCHELL:

We took Lily on her first train ride. Just a quick trip to Chinatown.

CAM:

I was worried she would think we were taking her back to Vietnam, but she seemed okay.

MITCHELL:

Yeah, yeah. Possibly because she was an infant when she left Vietnam. Also, Vietnam is not China.

CAM:

Well, I had a lollipop with me, just in case.

Season 3, Episode 7

MITCHELL:

Cam has this crazy theory that if he were straight, and Julia Roberts were single, they'd be dating.

CAM:

It's not crazy. I met her once at an AIDS walk, and our chemistry was palpable.

MITCHELL:

No, you handed her a bottle of water.

CAM:

And her fingers lingered.

MITCHELL:

Because you wouldn't let go.

cam *and* mitchell's

grilled fish tacos *with* lime crema *and* mango salsa

Serves 4

FOR THE MANGO SALSA:

1¾ cups diced peeled mango (about 2 mangoes)

¼ cup diced red onion

2 tablespoons chopped fresh cilantro

FOR THE LIME CREMA:

½ cup mayonnaise

½ cup fresh cilantro leaves

3 tablespoons fresh lime juice

½ ripe Hass avocado, peeled

FOR THE TACOS:

1 pound mahimahi

⅛ teaspoon kosher salt

⅛ teaspoon freshly ground black pepper

Cooking spray

8 corn tortillas, warmed

2 cups shredded red cabbage

1 Make the mango salsa: Combine all the ingredients in a bowl. Cover and refrigerate until ready to serve.

2 Make the lime crema: Put all the ingredients in a food processor; process until smooth. Cover and refrigerate for up to 2 days.

3 Make the tacos: Prepare a grill for cooking over medium-high heat.

4 Sprinkle the fish with the salt and pepper. Place the fish on the grill grate coated with cooking spray; cook for 5 minutes on each side or until the fish flakes easily when tested with a fork. Remove from the grill; break into chunks with a fork.

5 While the fish is cooking, warm the tortillas according to the package directions.

6 Divide the fish, salsa, and cabbage among the tortillas and drizzle each taco with 1½ tablespoons of the crema. Serve immediately.

claire's | pesto shrimp pasta

Serves 4

4 ounces uncooked angel hair pasta	**1 cup halved grape or cherry tomatoes**
1¼ pounds peeled and deveined large shrimp	**¼ cup (1 ounce) shaved Parmesan cheese**
4 tablespoons prepared pesto	**Fresh basil sprigs (optional)**

1 Cook the pasta according to the package directions, omitting salt and fat; drain.

2 While the pasta cooks, bring 6 cups water to a boil in a large saucepan. Add the shrimp; cook for 2 to 3 minutes or until opaque all the way through. Drain the shrimp; put in a large serving bowl and toss with 2 tablespoons of the pesto and the tomatoes. Stir in the pasta and the remaining 2 tablespoons pesto. Top with the cheese. Garnish with basil, if desired. Serve warm.

Clive—
Meet me in my room
xx Juliana

Season 6, Episode 14

PHIL:
I must say, Juliana, you're the last person I expected to see here tonight.

CLAIRE:
Well, with any luck, you'll be the last person I do see tonight.

PHIL:
Oh, my God.

CLAIRE:
Phil, I've had my eye on you for years. I'm just so happy we're finally gonna get some alone time. I'm not scaring you, am I?

PHIL:
Quite the contrary. Most women who meet me almost instantly ask for some alone time.

alex's | homemade fish sticks

Serves 6

Cooking spray

2 pounds skinless halibut fillets, cut into 1-inch-wide sticks

½ cup plain Greek yogurt

¼ cup sweet pickle relish

2 tablespoons fresh lemon juice

1 tablespoon milk

⅝ teaspoon kosher salt

4 ounces whole-wheat bread, crusts removed

1 cup all-purpose flour

1 cup buttermilk

½ teaspoon freshly ground black pepper

1 Preheat the oven to 425°F. Spray a baking sheet with cooking spray. Set aside.

2 Pop the fish into the freezer for 10 minutes while you prepare the other ingredients. You want the fish very, very cold but not fully frozen.

3 Combine the yogurt, relish, lemon juice, milk, and ⅛ teaspoon of the salt. Cover and chill in the refrigerator.

4 Pulse the bread in a food processor to make fine bread crumbs. Heat a large skillet over medium heat. Put the bread crumbs in the skillet and toast for 3 minutes, stirring frequently.

5 Ready a standard breading setup with three shallow dishes: flour, buttermilk, and bread crumbs. Remove the fish from the freezer and sprinkle with the remaining ½ teaspoon salt and the pepper. Coat the fish sticks in flour, then buttermilk (make sure there are no dry spots), and finally bread crumbs. Arrange the fish sticks on the prepared baking sheet, evenly spaced, and mist them evenly with cooking spray. Bake for 15 minutes or until the bread crumbs are crisp and the fish flakes easily when tested with a fork. Serve immediately, with the sweet pickle yogurt for dipping.

Season 2, Episode 5

ALEX, AFTER THE DUNPHYS MADE A BET TO SEE WHO COULD GO THE LONGEST WITHOUT ELECTRONICS:

How am I supposed to do my homework?

CLAIRE:

The way I did.

PHIL:

With a chisel and a piece of stone.

CLAIRE:

Phil.

PHIL:

You can't unplug my funny bone.

gloria's | latin chicken stew

Serves 6

- 2 baking potatoes (about 1½ pounds), peeled and cut into chunks (3⅓ cups)
- 1 (10-ounce) package frozen whole-kernel corn
- 2 stalks celery, chopped
- 2 carrots, peeled and cut into chunks (1 cup)
- 1 onion, cut into ½-inch-thick slices
- 2 garlic cloves, minced
- 1 cup bottled salsa
- 1½ teaspoons ground cumin

- 1 teaspoon chili powder
- ½ teaspoon freshly ground black pepper
- 1 pound skinless, boneless chicken breast
- 4 skinless, boneless chicken thighs (about 10½ ounces)
- 2½ cups low-sodium chicken broth
- 4 (6-inch) fresh corn tortillas, cut into strips
- Chopped fresh parsley (optional)

1 Put the potatoes, corn, celery, carrots, onion, and garlic in a slow cooker. Stir in the salsa, cumin, chili powder, and pepper. Place the chicken on top of the vegetables and add the broth. Cover and cook on the high setting for 4 hours.

2 Remove the chicken from the slow cooker; shred with two forks. Return the chicken to the slow cooker. Stir the tortilla strips into the stew. Garnish with parsley, if desired. Serve hot.

Season 3, Episode 5

GLORIA:

Okay. I'm going to tell you a story about a little girl who entered a beauty pageant, even though she was very, very scared that she was going to lose.

CLAIRE:

Let me guess. You won.

GLORIA:

Of course I won. But I was talking about my cousin, Maria Conchita. She had a nose like a toucan, she stuff her body in this bikini, and at the end, she finished dead last.

CLAIRE:

How is that a good story?

GLORIA:

She faced her fears, and it didn't kill her. What killed her two weeks later was a bus.

CAM:

I'm putting together a little scrapbook of how Lily became ours. You know, her adoption certificates and pictures of her from her village, all out in the open, so she has nothing to be ashamed of . . . and I'm also gonna write a little storybook . . . something I can read her at bedtime. It's called Two Monkeys and a Panda. She's the panda, because she's Asian.

MITCHELL:

And we're monkeys because . . . ?

CAM:

I can draw monkeys.

the tucker-pritchetts' | spicy asian noodles *with* chicken

Serves 4

- 3 teaspoons dark sesame oil
- 1 tablespoon grated peeled fresh ginger
- 2 garlic cloves, minced
- 2 cups chopped cooked skinless, boneless chicken breast
- ½ cup chopped green onions
- ¼ cup chopped fresh cilantro
- 3 tablespoons low-sodium soy sauce
- 2 tablespoons rice vinegar
- 2 tablespoons hoisin sauce
- 2 teaspoons chili paste with garlic (such as sambal oelek)
- 1 (6¾-ounce) package thin rice sticks (rice-flour noodles)
- 2 tablespoons chopped dry-roasted peanuts

1 Heat 2 teaspoons of the sesame oil in a small skillet over medium-high heat. Add the ginger and garlic to the pan; cook for 45 seconds, stirring constantly. Transfer to a large bowl. Stir in the remaining 1 teaspoon oil, the chicken, green onions, cilantro, soy sauce, rice vinegar, hoisin sauce, and chili paste.

2 Cook the noodles according to the package directions. Drain and rinse under cold water; drain again. Cut the noodles into smaller (2- to 4-inch) pieces. Add the noodles to the bowl; toss well to coat. Sprinkle with the peanuts.

TIP: To make prep even easier for busy nights, chop ginger and garlic in advance and freeze them in heaping-tablespoon-size mounds on a piece of waxed paper. Then pop the mounds in a freezer bag and they'll be ready to toss into the skillet when you need them.

Season 2, Episode 13

MITCHELL:

We love our neighborhood. But sometimes the last thing you wanna do after fighting traffic is get back in the car to go out to eat—and the only restaurant within walking distance is Shawarma City.

mitchell's | all-white-meat chicken shawarma

Serves 4 or 5

¼ cup tahini (sesame paste)

2 garlic cloves, minced

2 tablespoons fresh lemon juice

½ cup plain Greek yogurt

Kosher salt

2 tablespoons extra-virgin olive oil

1 large onion, cut into thin slivers

1 poblano pepper, seeded and thinly sliced

1½ tablespoons ground cumin

4 cups shredded rotisserie chicken breast (about 1 pound)

¼ cup chopped fresh parsley

Warmed pitas, chopped lettuce, and chopped tomatoes for serving

1 In a blender or mini chopper, combine the tahini with ½ cup water, half of the garlic, and the lemon juice and puree until smooth, adding more water 1 tablespoon at a time if necessary to achieve a thick but pourable sauce. Add the yogurt and process until creamy. Season with salt.

2 In a large bowl, combine the olive oil, onion, poblano, and cumin and season with salt. Heat a large griddle over high heat until nearly smoking. Add the vegetables and cook over high heat, stirring, until lightly charred and just tender, about 5 minutes. Add the chicken and parsley, season lightly with salt, and cook, stirring, just until heated through. Serve the shawarma with the tahini sauce, warmed pitas, and chopped lettuce and tomatoes.

cam *and* mitchell's | parmesan baked chicken

Season 4, Episode 9

CAM:

You know what? You're a list-maker, a planner. I'm a doer and an action-taker! Sean Penn would play me in a movie about this, or Anne Hathaway, if they wanted a female-driven vehicle.

MITCHELL:

And who would play your long-suffering partner?

CAM:

Julianne Moore, either way.

MITCHELL:

I would totally see that. I would.

Serves 4

⅓ cup Italian-seasoned bread crumbs

¼ cup grated Parmesan cheese

¼ teaspoon freshly ground black pepper

2 garlic cloves, pressed

2 tablespoons olive oil

4 (6-ounce) skinless, boneless chicken breast halves

Cooking spray

½ cup fire-roasted tomato-and-garlic pasta sauce (such as Classico), warmed

1 Preheat the oven to 425°F. Heat a large baking sheet in the oven for 5 minutes.

2 Combine the bread crumbs, cheese, and pepper in a shallow dish.

3 Put the garlic and oil in a small glass bowl and microwave on high power for 30 seconds or until warm and fragrant. Dip the chicken in the garlic oil; dredge in the bread-crumb mixture. Coat the preheated baking sheet with cooking spray and place the chicken on the pan. Coat the chicken with cooking spray. Bake for 25 minutes or until cooked through and golden. Serve hot, with the pasta sauce.

TIP: Preheating the baking sheet before putting the chicken on it makes the crust become extra crunchy.

See photo on following spread

the *dunphys'* | fail-safe roast chicken

Season 1, Episode 1

CLAIRE:

I was out of control growing up. There, you know, I said it. I just don't want my kids to make the same bad mistakes I made. If Haley never wakes up on a beach in Florida half-naked, I've done my job.

PHIL:

Our job.

CLAIRE:

Right. I've done our job.

Serves 4

1 (4-pound) whole chicken

¾ teaspoon kosher salt

¼ teaspoon freshly ground black pepper

2 tablespoons unsalted butter

2 teaspoons fresh lemon juice

2 teaspoons chopped fresh herbs, such as chives, tarragon, and basil

1 Preheat oven to 425°F.

2 Remove and discard the giblets and neck from the chicken. Trim excess fat. Tie the ends of the legs together with kitchen string. Lift the wing tips up and over the back; tuck them under the chicken. Sprinkle with ½ teaspoon of the salt and the pepper.

3 Place the chicken, breast side down, in a shallow roasting pan. Bake for 30 minutes. Turn the chicken over; baste with the pan drippings. Bake until a thermometer inserted into the meaty part of a leg registers 165°F, about an additional 20 minutes. Remove the chicken from the pan; let stand for 10 minutes. Carve the chicken.

4 Combine the butter and lemon juice in a small saucepan; cook over low heat for 2 minutes or until the butter melts. Remove from the heat; stir in the remaining ¼ teaspoon salt and the herbs. Serve the chicken with the sauce.

TIP: Use leftovers, if there are any, to make a single-serving version of Claire's potato-chip-enhanced sandwich on page 107.

phil's | honey-roasted cornish hen

Serves 2

1 **tablespoon honey, plus more for garnish (optional)**

1 **teaspoon chopped fresh oregano, plus 4 to 6 sprigs**

1 **teaspoon fresh lemon juice**

⅛ **teaspoon kosher salt**

⅛ **teaspoon freshly ground black pepper**

1 **(1-pound) Cornish hen, skinned, no giblets**

1 **lemon wedge, plus lemon slices for garnish (optional)**

Vegetable-oil cooking spray

½ **teaspoon vegetable oil**

1 Preheat the oven to 450°F.

2 Combine the honey, chopped oregano, lemon juice, salt, and pepper in a small bowl, stirring well; set aside.

3 Rinse the hen under cold water and pat dry. Place the oregano sprigs and lemon wedge in the cavity of the hen; close the cavity with skewers. Tie the ends of the legs together with kitchen string. Lift the wing tips up and over the back of the hen, tucking them under the bird. Place the hen, breast side up, on a rack in a roasting pan coated with cooking spray. Brush with the oil.

4 Place the hen in the oven and immediately lower the oven temperature to 350°F; bake for 35 minutes. Brush the hen with half of the honey mixture; bake for 10 minutes. Brush with the remaining honey mixture and bake for an additional 10 minutes or until the hen is cooked through and a thermometer inserted into the meaty part of a leg registers 165°F. Transfer the hen to a serving plate. If desired, drizzle additional honey on the serving plate and garnish with additional lemon slices and oregano sprigs. To serve, split the hen in half lengthwise, using an electric knife.

Hello my name is CLIVE BIXBY

Season 2, Episode 14

PHIL, AFTER TASTING CLAIRE'S DRINK AND SPITTING SOME OF IT BACK INTO HER GLASS:

Appletini?

CLAIRE:

It was. You're looking handsome as ever, Clive.

PHIL:

As you are, Juliana. You look hot enough to cook a pizza on . . . in . . . .

luke's | dino drumsticks

Season 2, Episode 21

LUKE:

You know more people have died hiking than in the entire Civil War?

ALEX:

Okay, what book did you read that in?

LUKE:

Book? Wake up and smell the Internet, Grandma.

Serves 6

6 **turkey drumsticks (about 1 pound each)**

4 **tablespoons unsalted butter, melted**

1 **teaspoon kosher salt**

1 **teaspoon freshly ground black pepper**

1 **teaspoon paprika**

1 **teaspoon ground coriander**

1 **teaspoon onion powder**

1 **teaspoon garlic powder**

1 **teaspoon dried thyme, rubbed**

1 Preheat the oven to 350°F.

2 Arrange the turkey legs in a roasting pan or large ovenproof skillet and rub with the melted butter. In a small bowl, combine the salt, pepper, paprika, coriander, onion powder, garlic powder, and thyme. Rub the spice mixture all over the drumsticks. Add 1 cup water to the pan and roast until an instant-read thermometer inserted into the thickest part of a drumstick registers 170°F, about 1 hour 15 minutes, adding water to the pan as necessary to keep it from drying out. Serve.

luke *and* phil's
INVENTION MATRIX

Like father, like son: Phil and Luke are a pair of modern da Vincis. They're always coming up with inventions that startle and delight (mostly startle, if you ask Claire). Here are some of their zaniest ideas.

• Blimps Tethered to Mailboxes

CLAIRE: So the only reason we don't have a blimp tethered to our mailbox is because *I'm* always shooting down *your* great ideas?

PHIL: Well...

• Self-Flipping Pancakes

PHIL: If this works, centuries from now, someone's gonna dig one of these things up and wonder what the heck it is.

Asprin Gun •

CLAIRE: The aspirin gun.

PHIL: Some people have a hard time swallowing.

AwesomeLand •

CLAIRE: Welcome to AwesomeLand, where the only thing to fear is fun itself.

• Shower Snacks

PHIL: You veto me all the time.

CLAIRE: 'Cause you have dumb ideas.

PHIL: Name one. (PAUSE) That went on for a while.

CLAIRE: . . . and let's not forget shower snacks.

PHIL: I can't be the only one who gets hungry in there!

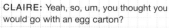
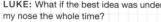

useless ←

Adult Tricycles •

CLAIRE: Adult tricycles.

PHIL: Just try to fall off.

• Luke's Egg Dropper

LUKE: I have to design a container that'll protect an egg in a one-story drop.

CLAIRE: Yeah, so, um, you thought you would go with an egg carton?

LUKE: What if the best idea was under my nose the whole time?

• Dunphy Towers

LUKE: Look what I built, Dad. Dunphy Towers. Two hundred condos, a happy family in every one.

PHIL: Way to go, buddy. (TO CLAIRE) I gotta hand it to you, honey. Twenty-four hours without video games, he's already contributing to society.

LUKE, PUMMELING DUNPHY TOWERS WITH A BASEBALL BAT: Die! Die!

Rice Pudding • Franchise

CLAIRE: Ha-ha. Let's review the squelch pile, Phil. Let's see, the rice pudding franchise.

PHIL: Works for all chewing abilities.

Coffee Bot

ALEX: Where's the coffeepot?

LUKE: Oh, you mean the soon-to-be coffee bot?

Auto-Buttering Toaster

LUKE: If only the springs were stronger, the toast would be catapulted into the pool of butter.

PHIL: Really strong springs, like the ones in your mattress?

Toy Truck Explorer

PHIL: See how much better this is? The truck goes in, it gets video, and then we get a preview of whatever's in there. How ingenious is that, huh?

LUKE: Are you too scared to go in?

PHIL: What? Why would you say that?

LUKE: Well, when you stuck your head in you screamed a little.

Real Head-Scratcher

PHIL: The Real Head-Scratcher features thirty-two patent-pending "nogginizers" that gently massage your scalp in a soothing purr of motorized delight.

LUKE: Ohh, that feels great. And it looks good, too. It's a real lifesaver.

PHIL: You mean a Real Head-Scratcher?

Drone

PHIL: That "thing" is a professional aerial-photography tool for real-estate use only!

CLAIRE: You used it at the beach to film yourself doing sand angels.

PHIL: For my "Phil Dunphy Will Get You a Heavenly Deal on a Beach House" video.

The Phillowcase

PHIL: "Gil pickles." Genius. So much better than my Phillowcases. Claire wasn't a fan.

Rest Assured

Iron for Grilled Cheese

MANNY: Okay, let me just say what everyone's thinking: My jacket's a mess. It wouldn't be, but someone used the iron to make grilled cheese.

LUKE: I had bread, I had cheese, and I had an iron. What was I supposed to do?

the *dunphys'* | roast turkey *with* sausage–corn bread stuffing

Season 6, Episode 8

PHIL:

I am cooking Thanksgiving dinner this year. Huge step for Claire to trust me with this. But I have help— this new app. It's, uh, international superchef Nigella Lawson. I can even program my name, so it's like she's right here guiding my every move with that sultry British voice. I listened to her meringue instructions in the car last week. There was so much whipping and beating, I had to pull over.

Serves 16 to 24

1 (12- to 14-pound) turkey	½ teaspoon kosher salt
Sausage–Corn Bread Stuffing with Giblets (recipe follows)	½ teaspoon freshly ground black pepper
2 tablespoons unsalted butter or margarine, melted	2 tablespoons all-purpose flour

1 Remove the giblets and neck from the turkey; set aside. Rinse the turkey with cold water; pat dry. Cover and refrigerate while preparing the stuffing.

2 Preheat the oven to 450°F.

3 Stuff the stuffing loosely into the cavity of the turkey; close with skewers. Tie the ends of the legs to the tail with kitchen string, or tuck them under a band of skin at the tail. Lift the wing tips up and over the back, tucking them under the bird securely.

4 Brush the entire bird with the melted butter; sprinkle with the salt and pepper. Rub the flour over the surface of the turkey. Place breast side up on a rack in a roasting pan; pour 2 cups water in the bottom of the pan. Bake for 30 minutes, then lower the oven temperature to 325°F and bake for 3 hours. Cut the string or band of skin holding the drumstick ends to the tail. Continue baking for an additional 30 minutes to 1 hour or until the drumsticks are easy to move and a thermometer inserted into the stuffing registers at least 165°F.

5 Transfer the turkey to a serving platter. Let stand for at least 15 minutes before carving. Serve warm.

sausage–corn bread stuffing *with* giblets

Makes 9 cups (enough for a 12- to 14-pound turkey)

Giblets reserved from turkey

6 cups corn-bread crumbs

6 slices bread, cut into 1-inch cubes

½ teaspoon kosher salt

½ teaspoon freshly ground black pepper

½ cup (1 stick) unsalted butter or margarine

½ pound bulk pork sausage

2 cups chopped celery

1 medium onion, finely chopped

"You only get one chance at a first impression. I suggest Julia Child, because it's easy to do: 'Save the giblets!'"

—PHIL

1 Put the giblets in a saucepan with 2 cups water; cover and simmer for 1 to 2 hours or until they are tender. Remove giblets from the broth, reserving 1 cup broth. Chop the giblets; set aside.

2 Combine the corn-bread crumbs and bread cubes in a large mixing bowl; add ¼ cup water, the salt, and the pepper. Set aside.

3 Melt the butter in a large skillet; add the sausage, celery, and onion. Sauté for 3 minutes. Cover and cook for an additional 30 minutes or until the sausage is browned and the vegetables are tender; stir frequently. Remove from the heat; stir into the bread mixture. Add the reserved giblet broth and giblets, mixing well.

NOTE: If you prefer, you can bake the stuffing in a separate buttered or oiled baking dish until heated through and crusty.

BAKED GOODS *and* DESSERTS

Season 5, Episode 3

PHIL:

How about that master suite, huh?

LORRAINE:

Maybe if I had someone to share it with.

PHIL:

Lorraine, you are a beautiful woman with a lot to offer. Should we *make* an offer?

lorraine's | zucchini bread

Makes 1 (9-by-5-inch) loaf

Cooking spray

1 cup packed shredded zucchini

1 cup packed light brown sugar

2 large eggs

¾ cup buttermilk

4 tablespoons unsalted butter, melted

1 teaspoon vanilla extract

2 cups all-purpose flour

1 tablespoon baking powder

1 teaspoon baking soda

1 teaspoon ground cinnamon

½ teaspoon ground cloves

¼ teaspoon kosher salt

1 Preheat the oven to 350°F. Coat a 9-by-5-inch loaf pan with cooking spray.

2 Press the zucchini between several layers of paper towels; cover with additional paper towels. Let stand for 5 minutes, pressing down occasionally, to remove excess water.

3 Combine the brown sugar and eggs in a large bowl; beat well with a wooden spoon. Stir in the zucchini, buttermilk, melted butter, and vanilla.

4 Combine the flour, baking powder, baking soda, cinnamon, cloves, and salt in a medium bowl. Gradually add to the zucchini mixture, stirring just until the flour mixture is moist. Spread the batter in the prepared loaf pan. Bake for 53 to 55 minutes or until a toothpick inserted in the center comes out clean. Let cool in the pan on a wire rack for 10 minutes; remove from the pan and let cool completely on the wire rack.

phil's | banana bread

Season 5, Episode 17

PHIL:

Ohh, I am the king of banana bread. You know my secret? No nuts.

JAY:

Not such a secret.

Makes 1 (8-by-4-inch) loaf

Cooking spray

1 cup whole-wheat flour

½ cup all-purpose flour

1 teaspoon baking powder

1 teaspoon baking soda

⅛ teaspoon kosher salt

¼ cup "measures-like-sugar" calorie-free sweetener

2 tablespoons unsalted butter or margarine, melted

4 medium very ripe bananas, peeled and mashed

1 large egg, lightly beaten

1 Preheat the oven to 350°F. Coat an 8-by-4-inch loaf pan with cooking spray.

2 Combine the flours, baking powder, baking soda, and salt in a large bowl.

3 Combine the sweetener, melted butter, bananas, and egg in a medium bowl; add to the flour mixture, stirring just until moist. Pour the batter into the prepared pan. Bake for 50 to 55 minutes or until a toothpick inserted in the center comes out clean. Let cool in the pan on a wire rack for 10 minutes; remove from the pan and let cool completely on the wire rack.

"No one insults my banana bread!"

— PHIL

PHIL, AFTER RUNNING INTO TWO
CLIENTS AT THE SUPERMARKET:

I'm both your Realtors.
I-I'm just lucky to have
such a—

LORRAINE:

We're on our way to an
open house.

DIANE:

Oh, is that why you
couldn't show me the
Colonial later? I made that
corn bread that you like.

PHIL:

W-we're gonna make it
to that. I just have to finish
up with Lorraine.

LORRAINE:

Oh, you mean, like,
"get it over with"?

PHIL:

No, I-I don't mean that.

LORRAINE:

And I thought zucchini
bread was your favorite . . .
Why am I buying zucchini?

PHIL:

Hey, can't a guy like
zucchini bread *and* corn
bread?

diane's | corn bread

Makes 1 (9-by-9-inch) loaf

1 **cup all-purpose flour**   2 **large eggs, beaten**
1 **cup yellow cornmeal**   1 **cup milk**
4 **teaspoons baking powder**   ¼ **cup vegetable oil**
¾ **teaspoon kosher salt**

1 Preheat the oven to 425°F. Generously oil a 9-inch square baking pan.

2 Combine the flour, cornmeal, baking powder, and salt in a large mixing
bowl; stir well.

3 Combine the eggs, milk, and oil in a small mixing bowl, mixing until well
blended. Slowly pour over the cornmeal mixture, stirring just until the dry
ingredients are moistened. Pour the batter into the prepared pan. Bake for
20 minutes or until lightly browned and a toothpick inserted in the center
comes out clean. Cut into squares and serve warm or at room temperature.

andy's | flaxseed muffins

Makes 12

Cooking spray

¼ cup plus 2 tablespoons whole flaxseeds

1½ cups all-purpose flour

2¼ teaspoons baking powder

½ cup loosely packed light brown sugar

1 teaspoon ground cinnamon

½ teaspoon freshly grated nutmeg

⅛ teaspoon ground cloves

¾ teaspoon kosher salt

1 cup milk

1 large egg, beaten

1 teaspoon vanilla extract

¼ cup plus 2 tablespoons canola oil

1 cup toasted walnuts, coarsely chopped (3 ounces)

2 tablespoons turbinado sugar

1 Preheat the oven to 375°F. Spray a 12-cup standard muffin tin with cooking spray (vegetable oil with flour).

2 Put ¼ cup of the flaxseeds into a coffee grinder and pulse until coarsely ground. Transfer to a medium bowl and whisk in the flour, baking powder, brown sugar, cinnamon, nutmeg, cloves, and salt.

3 In a small bowl, whisk the milk with the egg, vanilla, and oil. Add the liquid ingredients to the dry ingredients along with the walnuts and fold just until moistened. Divide the batter among the prepared muffin cups, filling them three-quarters full. Sprinkle with the remaining 2 tablespoons whole flaxseeds and the turbinado sugar and bake in the center of the oven until springy and golden, 18 to 20 minutes. Let cool slightly on a rack, then turn the muffins out onto a platter and serve. The muffins can be refrigerated in an airtight container for up to 3 days and rewarmed, wrapped in foil, before serving.

TIP: Wrap leftovers in plastic, put them in a freezer bag, and freeze them; pack one for lunch or an afternoon snack.

Season 5, Episode 6

ANDY, AS BELL DINGS:

Those are the flaxseed muffins that I just baked. I'll just take them out and get out of here.

JAY:

Andy, wait. We're never gonna eat them.

gloria's | buñuelos

Makes 24

2 cups (8 ounces) Colombian queso costeño, or 1½ cups queso fresco and ½ cup ricotta salata

1¼ cups cornstarch

¼ cup yucca flour (tapioca or cassava starch)

2 tablespoons sugar

1 tablespoon baking powder

2 large eggs, beaten

¼ cup milk

Vegetable oil for frying

Confectioners' sugar for dusting (optional)

1 Pulse the cheese in a food processor until it is finely chopped and resembles coarse meal. Transfer to a large, wide bowl and whisk in the cornstarch, yucca flour, sugar, and baking powder. Add the eggs and the milk and stir until moistened. Using your hands, gently knead the dough in the bowl until evenly combined. The dough should be smooth and firm but not dry. Roll the dough into 24 (1½-inch) balls and transfer to a waxed paper–lined baking sheet.

2 Fill a large Dutch oven with 2 inches of vegetable oil and heat the oil to 325°F. Fry the buñuelos in two or three batches over medium heat, turning occasionally, until golden all over and cooked through, about 8 minutes. Be sure the oil doesn't get too hot, or the outside will brown before the inside is done. Drain on a paper towel–lined baking sheet and let cool for 15 minutes. Dust with confectioners' sugar, if desired, and serve warm.

NOTE: Yucca flour (aka tapioca flour or cassava starch) can often be found in the gluten-free baking section of the supermarket.

Season 1, Episode 10

GLORIA:

Where were you for so long?

JAY:

Just a little last-minute shopping…What's this?

MANNY:

Buñuelos.

JAY:

Who-what?

GLORIA:

Cheese fritters. It's a Colombian traditional Christmas food.

cam's | coffee-frosted brownies

Season 1, Episode 3

CAM:

I'm sort of like Costco. I'm big, I'm not fancy, and I dare you to not like me.

MITCHELL:

And I'm more like . . . that, um, what is the name of that little shop we went to in Paris?

CAM:

You are such a snob.

Makes 16

1¼ cups all-purpose flour

1 cup quick-cooking rolled oats

½ cup firmly packed brown sugar

⅓ cup unsalted butter, melted, plus ⅓ cup unmelted

1 tablespoon instant coffee granules

¼ teaspoon kosher salt

2 (1-ounce) squares unsweetened chocolate

2 large eggs

1 cup granulated sugar

2 tablespoons Kahlúa or other coffee-flavored liqueur

¾ cup toasted, chopped walnuts

Coffee Frosting (recipe follows)

Plain or chocolate-covered espresso beans (optional)

1 Combine ½ cup of the flour, the oats, brown sugar, ⅓ cup melted butter, the coffee granules, and salt in a medium bowl; stir well. Press the mixture into the bottom of an ungreased 9-inch square baking pan. Bake for 12 minutes, then remove to a rack; leave the oven on.

2 Combine the remaining ⅓ cup butter and the chocolate in a small saucepan. Cook over medium-low heat, stirring frequently, until melted. Let cool.

3 Beat the eggs with an electric mixer on medium speed until thick and pale. Add the granulated sugar and Kahlúa, beating until blended. Stir in the chocolate mixture, the remaining ¾ cup flour, and the walnuts; spread the mixture evenly over the crust. Bake for 25 minutes. Let cool completely in the pan on a wire rack.

4 Spread the frosting over the brownies. Cover and let stand until the frosting hardens. Cut into 16 squares. Garnish with the espresso beans, if desired.

continued on next page

coffee frosting

Makes 1 cup

⅓ cup unsalted butter or margarine, softened

2¼ cups sifted confectioners' sugar

1½ tablespoons Kahlúa or other coffee-flavored liqueur

2 tablespoons finely chopped chocolate-covered espresso beans

1 Beat the butter with an electric mixer on medium speed until creamy. Gradually add the confectioners' sugar and Kahlúa, beating until blended. Fold in the chocolate-covered espresso beans.

NOTE: Chocolate-covered coffee beans are available at specialty food shops or gourmet candy counters. Substitute cold brewed coffee for Kahlúa, if desired.

"Is that one of Claire's brownies?"
"No, it's delicious. Must be Cam's."

—GLORIA & JAY

claire's | pumpkin pie *with* vanilla whipped cream

Makes 1 (9-inch) pie; serves 10

1 cup plus 2 tablespoons sugar

1 teaspoon ground cinnamon

½ teaspoon kosher salt

½ teaspoon ground ginger

¼ teaspoon ground cloves

2 large eggs

1 (15-ounce) can pumpkin puree

¾ cup evaporated milk

1 ball Pastry Dough (page 215), or ½ (14.1-ounce) package refrigerated pie dough

½ cup heavy cream, chilled

½ teaspoon vanilla extract

1 Preheat the oven to 425°F.

2 Combine 1 cup of the sugar, the cinnamon, salt, ginger, and cloves in a large bowl; stir well with a whisk. Add the eggs and pumpkin; stir well with the whisk. Whisk in the evaporated milk.

3 Fit the dough into a 9-inch pie plate. Fold the edges under. Pour in the pumpkin mixture.

4 Place the pie plate on a baking sheet and bake for 15 minutes; reduce the oven temperature to 350°F and bake for an additional 45 minutes or until the filling is almost set in the center. Shield the edges of the piecrust with foil, if necessary. (Do not insert a knife to test for doneness, as the slit will become larger and separate when the pie cools.) Let cool on a wire rack for 1½ hours.

5 Beat the cream with a mixer on high speed until foamy. Gradually add the vanilla and the remaining 2 tablespoons sugar, beating until soft peaks form. Slice the pie into 10 slices; top each serving with whipped cream.

Season 3, Episode 9

CLAIRE, UPSET THAT EVERYONE GETS UP TO LEAVE BEFORE EATING THANKSGIVING DINNER:

No, no, no, no! No, no, no! I did not just cook for eight hours so you people could run off to prove some asinine point that's only going to make half of us feel bad. Come on. Show a little respect.

JAY, AFTER THEY ALL COME BACK AND SIT AT THE TABLE:

Turkey smells great, sweetheart.

PHIL:

Is it turkey? Because something smells like chicken.

luke *and* phil's | doughnut waffle sundaes

Serves 4

4 slices bacon

½ cup pecan halves, coarsely chopped

½ cup maple syrup

4 glazed doughnuts

1 pint vanilla ice cream

1 In a skillet, cook the bacon over medium-high heat until crisp, 6 to 8 minutes, turning once. Drain on paper towels and let cool. Crumble finely. Add the pecans to the fat in the skillet and cook over medium heat, stirring, until toasted, about 5 minutes. Using a slotted spoon, drain the pecans on paper towels, reserving the bacon fat in the skillet.

2 In a small saucepan, bring the maple syrup to a boil. Add the bacon and pecans.

3 Preheat a waffle maker and brush it with bacon fat. Place a doughnut in the center of each section, close the waffle maker, and cook until toasted and caramelized, 2 to 3 minutes.

4 Arrange the donut waffles on plates and top each with a scoop of ice cream. Top with the syrup and serve right away.

Season 4, Episode 5

LUKE:

Why are there giant lollipops all over the front yard? And why do they taste so bad?

ALEX:

Because they're made out of cardboard, mouth-breather.

PHIL:

Hey, the world needs more dreamers, Luke. Never stop licking things.

HALEY:

Mom, why are you freaking out on everyone?

CLAIRE:

Because you are acting very irresponsibly. All of you. Listen, honey, Luke has a giant project due tomorrow for school that he hasn't even started, and Haley just informed me she needs forty cupcakes for her school fund-raiser, also due tomorrow.

ALEX:

I'd like to point out I completed all my assignments on my own and on time.

CLAIRE AND PHIL:

Not now, Alex.

haley's | buttercream cupcakes

Makes 48

3 cups sugar	1 cup vegetable oil
4½ cups all-purpose flour	8 large eggs, at room temperature
½ cup cornstarch	2 cups milk
5 teaspoons baking powder	1 tablespoon vanilla extract
1 teaspoon kosher salt	White Buttercream Frosting (recipe follows)
1 cup (2 sticks) unsalted butter, melted	

1 Preheat the oven to 350°F. Line four 12-cup muffin tins with paper liners. Arrange the oven racks in the lower and upper thirds of the oven.

2 In a large bowl, whisk the sugar, flour, cornstarch, baking powder, and salt. In a small bowl, combine the melted butter and oil.

3 Add the wet mixture to the dry mixture and, using a handheld electric mixer or large whisk, beat on low speed until smooth. Add the eggs, beating until combined, then add the milk and vanilla and beat until smooth, scraping the bottom and sides of the bowl. Transfer the batter to a pitcher and fill the muffin cups three-quarters full. Bake (in batches if necessary) until springy and a toothpick inserted in the center comes out clean, about 20 minutes. Let cool slightly, then transfer the cupcakes to a wire rack to cool completely.

4 Frost the cupcakes. The cupcakes can be wrapped or put in an airtight container and stored at room temperature for up to 2 days or frozen for up to 1 month.

continued on next page

white buttercream frosting

Makes about 5 cups (enough to frost 48 cupcakes)

1½ cups (3 sticks) unsalted butter, softened

8 cups confectioners' sugar, sifted

1 tablespoon vanilla extract

½ teaspoon kosher salt

¼ cup plus 2 tablespoons heavy cream

1 In a large bowl of a standing mixer fitted with the whisk attachment, beat the butter on medium speed until smooth. Add the confectioners' sugar, vanilla, and salt and beat on low speed just until combined. Increase the speed to medium and beat until smooth. Add the cream and beat until light and fluffy, about 2 minutes. The frosting can be stored, covered at room temperature, for up to 2 days.

"Do we still have the number to Poison Control?"

— CLAIRE

luke's | easy oatmeal–chocolate chip cookies

Makes about 72

- 2 cups all-purpose flour
- 1 teaspoon baking soda
- ½ teaspoon baking powder
- ½ teaspoon kosher salt
- 2 cups quick-cooking rolled oats
- 1 cup granulated sugar

- 1 cup firmly packed light brown sugar
- 1 cup chopped pecans
- 1 cup (6 ounces) semisweet chocolate chips
- 1 cup vegetable oil
- 2 large eggs, beaten
- 1 teaspoon vanilla extract

1 Preheat the oven to 350°F.

2 Stir together the flour, baking soda, baking powder, salt, oats, sugars, pecans, and chocolate chips in a large bowl. Add the oil, eggs, and vanilla; stir well. Shape the dough into 1-inch balls. (The dough will be crumbly.) Place the balls on ungreased baking sheets. Bake for 10 minutes or until golden. Let cool on the baking sheets for 1 minute; remove to wire racks to cool completely.

Season 3, Episode 16

LUKE:
We'll use these cookies as bait. Lily's crazy for them. . . . When she grabs them with her grubby little hands, off goes the trap. Boom—big puddle of milk. She'll get in so much trouble. My mom hates messes.

MANNY:
I'm familiar with Claire.

"We used to be the cute ones. Now she gets all of the attention.
We need to take her down."

—LUKE

cake-tastrophes

Cakes are the universal language of love, but parties never go the way they're planned on *Modern Family*. From botched birthdays to contagious weddings, these are some of the Dunphy-Tucker-Pritchett-Delgados' most traumatic (and satisfying) cake catastrophes.

The Cake Fair to Remember

The Hollywood-themed, fondant-covered cake Manny made for his school fair was a shoo-in for first place, even after Gloria sabotaged it and Manny was forced to turn the mess into a natural disaster–style "earthcake." He didn't win the blue ribbon, but the rage he displayed toward his elderly cake-baking rival did earn him a spot on Cam's football team, so this one still goes in the W column.

The Cake Topper That Never Topped the Cake

As soon as Mitchell ran out of wedding planning vetoes, Cam produced a cake topper that his father carved out of soap. It depicted a hulking, manly Cam and a stereotypically gay Mitchell. Letting Lily use it in the bathtub didn't destroy it, so Mitchell asked Jay to give it to Stella to bury in the backyard. Ultimately Cam dug it up and gave Mitchell one more veto, just so *he* could get one more veto, which he used to immediately ax Mitchell's choice for wedding singer.

The Cake That Caused the Plague

Everyone blamed Cam and Mitchell for spreading a virus around the family after they returned from their honeymoon with the flu, but it turned out that Phil was the real patient zero. (While editing video footage of the wedding, Phil saw himself on film sneezing onto the cake.) Rather than confess, Phil opted to set up a green screen to create the postproduction illusion that he was laughing near the cake—not coughing onto it. In the end, his creative editing was for nothing. Lily had witnessed the original crime, and she called him out in front of the entire family

The Cake That Got Away

When the Dunphy-Tucker-Pritchett-Delgados tried to plan an elaborate birthday dinner for Jay—even though he specifically asked to spend the day fishing alone—a variety of birthday-related disasters ensued. The low point was probably when Stella leapt up to the kitchen counter and pulled Jay's cake to the floor so she could eat a slice. At least someone enjoyed the celebration.

The Electronically Generated Doohickey Cake

Claire's plan to create the perfect birthday for Phil failed miserably. First, she overslept and missed her chance to buy him an iPad. Then, when he went to the batting cage to re-create his epic eleventh birthday—the one where he hit ten straight fastballs and made all his friends laugh when his buddy got hit in the groin with a curveball—he accidentally crashed a little kid's perfect birthday party. (His name was Phil too, and at least he had a cake.) Luckily, Luke saved the day by emailing a buddy of Phil's, who brought an iPad right over. Phil got to blow out the candles on his new birthday cake app.

Season 4, Episode 13

LILY:

I'm bored.

CAM:

I know, sweetie. But Daddies are talking about what we're gonna wear tonight . . . and that's a difficult conversation.

LILY:

Cry me a river.

MITCHELL:

Lily! I-I'm not loving this attitude. You seem a little mean.

LILY:

Sorry. Should I call you a waaahmbulance?

lily's | pineapple cake

Makes 1 (8-inch) 2-layer cake

½ cup vegetable shortening

1½ cups sugar

2 large eggs

2 cups all-purpose flour

2 teaspoons baking powder

¼ teaspoon baking soda

1 cup buttermilk

1 teaspoon vanilla extract

Pineapple Custard (recipe follows)

Chopped fresh pineapple (optional)

1 Preheat the oven to 350°F. Grease and flour two 8-inch round cake pans.

2 Beat the shortening with an electric mixer on high speed in a medium bowl; gradually add the sugar, beating well. Add the eggs, one at a time, beating well after each addition.

3 Combine the flour, baking powder, and baking soda in a medium bowl. Add the flour mixture to the sugar mixture alternately with the buttermilk, beginning and ending with the flour mixture. Stir in the vanilla. Pour the batter into the prepared pans. Bake for 35 minutes or until a toothpick inserted in the center comes out clean. Let cool in the pans for 10 minutes; remove from the pans to cool completely on a wire rack.

4 Spread the custard between the layers and on top of the cake. If you like, top the cake with fresh pineapple.

pineapple custard

Makes enough filling and topping for 1 (8-inch) 2-layer cake

1 cup evaporated milk

1 cup sugar

3 large egg yolks

½ cup (1 stick) unsalted butter or margarine

1 teaspoon vanilla extract

1 (20-ounce) can crushed pineapple, well drained and squeezed dry

1 Combine the evaporated milk, sugar, egg yolks, and butter in a heavy saucepan. Cook over medium heat, stirring constantly, until the mixture thickens to a thick pudding consistency. Stir in the vanilla and pineapple; mix well. Let cool completely.

lily's easy diva tips

Being a diva is about more than trendy threads and snappy one-liners, and no one knows that better than Lily Tucker-Pritchett. Whether she's kicking out interlopers her dads have accidentally invited to live with them, framing her baby cousin for crimes he didn't commit, or extorting the tooth fairy, Lily gets what Lily wants. You, too, can find your inner diva by following her tried-and-true advice.

1   **Choose a killer outfit.**
Maybe it's a tiara? Maybe it's Old Hollywood glam. Maybe it's a light-up lace hat. Maybe it's a Lizbo the Clown costume. Whatever makes you feel super fab, wear it and own it.

2   **Know what you want.**
Are you hungry? Lie on top of the car hood and refuse to move. Are you at a Vietnamese restaurant? Order a cheeseburger anyway.

3   **Never settle.**
You're a diva! You deserve to be treated like royalty! Set your sights on a man who likes the swings, sits by the flag, and can count to a hundred.

4   **Master your sass.**
If someone's hair is weird, tell them. If you're bored, say so. If your parents are whining, offer to call them a waaahmbulance. Melodrama is an essential part of being a diva.

5   **Recognize game.**
Beyoncé's got nothing on you, but sometimes you'll find a formidable diva like Larry the Cat. Call him crazy, but he's the one who gets to sleep on the solid-white designer couch.

6   **Never back down.**
When someone tells you you can't go as Belle to your dads' wedding, remind them she faced the Beast and stood up to the townspeople!

7   **Fake it till you make it.**
Can't read? Stare at that paper anyway, girl. Can't sing? Pretend you're doing it on purpose to torture your dad. But then get in there and figure it out. Tell the world, "Got to go! Can't wait to learn!"

mitchell's | rosemary-infused grapefruit compote

Serves 10

1 cup sugar

3 tablespoons honey

3 sprigs fresh rosemary, plus more for garnish (optional)

6 large grapefruit

½ cup maraschino cherries with stems

1 Combine the sugar, ½ cup water, the honey, and rosemary in a saucepan. Bring to a boil over medium heat. Boil for 5 minutes. Remove from the heat and let cool completely. Remove and discard the rosemary.

2 Peel and section the grapefruit over a serving bowl to catch the juice. Add the grapefruit to the bowl. Pour in the rosemary syrup. Add the cherries. Cover and chill in the refrigerator until ready to serve. Garnish with fresh rosemary, if desired.

Season 4, Episode 10

CAM:

Mitchell, do you know what I've realized?

MITCHELL:

That some thoughts are better left unexpressed?

CAM:

No. That in this relationship, I'm the gas pedal, and you're the brakes.

MITCHELL:

Okay, wait, wait, wait, wait, wait. Last week you said that you were the painting, and I was the frame.

CAM:

That's if we were artwork. This is if we were a car.

MITCHELL:

I know what part you'd be if we were a horse.

claire's | brown sugar icebox cookies

Makes 24

1 cup all-purpose flour
¼ teaspoon baking soda
⅛ teaspoon salt
¼ cup unsalted butter, softened

⅔ cup packed brown sugar
1 teaspoon vanilla extract
1 large egg white
Cooking spray

1 Combine the flour, baking soda, and salt in a small bowl.

2 In a medium bowl, with an electric mixer, beat the butter at medium speed until light and fluffy. Gradually add the brown sugar, beating until well blended. Add the vanilla and egg white; beat well. Add the flour mixture and stir until well blended. Turn the dough out onto waxed paper; shape into a 6-inch log. Wrap the log in the waxed paper and freeze for 3 hours, or until very firm.

3 Preheat the oven to 350°F. Coat a baking sheet with cooking spray.

4 Cut the dough log into 24 (¼-inch) slices and place the slices 1 inch apart on the prepared baking sheet. Bake for 8 to 10 minutes, until lightly browned. Remove from the baking sheet and let cool on wire racks.

TIP: Double the recipe and keep one log in the freezer for cookie emergencies.

Season 1, Episode 3

MANNY:
Those cookies smell like heaven. Your own recipe?

CLAIRE:
No, I just throw 'em in the oven.

MANNY:
And added the secret ingredient of caring?

CLAIRE:
Sure.

luke's | rhubarb pie

Makes 1 (9-inch) pie

Pastry Dough (recipe follows)

Flour for the work surface

1½ cups plus 2 tablespoons sugar

2 tablespoons cornstarch

½ teaspoon freshly grated nutmeg

½ cup fresh orange juice

6 cups sliced rhubarb

2 tablespoons unsalted butter or margarine

1 egg white, beaten

1 Preheat the oven to 450°F.

2 Flour a work surface and roll one of the dough balls into a circle ⅛ inch thick; fit into a 9-inch pie plate, leaving overhang.

3 Combine 1½ cups of the sugar, the cornstarch, and nutmeg in a medium saucepan; stir the mixture to remove lumps. Stir in the orange juice. Cook over medium heat, stirring constantly, until the mixture thickens. Remove from the heat. Add the rhubarb and butter, stirring until the butter melts. Spoon the rhubarb mixture into the prepared pastry shell.

4 Roll the remaining dough ball to a circle with ⅛-inch thickness and cut into fourteen 10-by-½-inch strips. Arrange the strips in a lattice fashion over the filling; press the ends gently to seal the strips to the pastry overhang. Trim and flute the edges. Brush the lattice and rim with the egg white and sprinkle with the remaining 2 tablespoons sugar. Bake for 10 minutes; reduce the oven temperature to 350°F and bake for an additional 30 minutes or until the crust is lightly browned. Let cool completely before serving.

pastry dough

Makes enough dough for 1 (9-inch) lattice-top pie, or 2 (9-inch) single-crust pies

2 cups all-purpose flour

½ teaspoon kosher salt

⅔ cup plus 2 tablespoons vegetable shortening

5 to 6 tablespoons ice-cold water

1 Sift the flour and salt into a large bowl; cut in the shortening with a pastry blender until the mixture resembles coarse meal. Sprinkle in the water and stir with a fork. Shape into two balls, wrap in plastic, and refrigerate for 30 minutes.

Season 6, Episode 1

MITCHELL:

Hey, guys.

LUKE:

Sweet! You brought the sifter. Aw! Now I can start my rhubarb pie.

HALEY:

Ooh, can I help pick the rhubarb?

LUKE:

Lead the way, kitten.

claire *and* phil's | cherry clafouti

Season 1, Episode 8

PHIL:

Heey, coupons for . . .
five free hugs.

CLAIRE:

You don't like it.

PHIL:

Are you kidding me?
I love it. It's so . . . creative.
Coupons for hugs, which
are usually free, but this
makes it official, which
is so great.

Serves 12

1 tablespoon unsalted butter, softened

6 large eggs

1¼ cups milk

½ cup granulated sugar

2 tablespoons brandy

1 tablespoon vanilla extract

¼ teaspoon kosher salt

⅔ cup all-purpose flour

1 pint (2 heaping cups) pitted black cherries, stemmed; or 1 (12-ounce) package frozen cherries, thawed

Confectioners' sugar (optional)

1 Preheat the oven to 400°F. Generously coat a 10-inch cast-iron skillet or glass pie dish with the butter.

2 Process the eggs, milk, sugar, brandy, vanilla, and salt in a blender until well blended. Add the flour and process until the batter is smooth and well blended.

3 Scatter the cherries in the prepared skillet and pour the batter over them. Bake until puffed and golden, about 30 minutes. Lightly dust with confectioners' sugar, if desired. Serve warm or at room temperature.

manny's | chocolate torte

Makes 1 (8-inch) torte

- **4 tablespoons unsalted butter, cut into pieces, plus more for the pan**
- **½ cup all-purpose flour, plus more for dusting**
- **2 tablespoons unsweetened cocoa powder, sifted, for dusting**
- **6 ounces bittersweet chocolate (72%), broken into pieces**
- **3 tablespoons brewed espresso**
- **1 teaspoon vanilla extract**
- **½ cup plus 2 tablespoons granulated sugar**
- **3 large eggs, separated**
- **Confectioners' sugar, for dusting**
- **Sweetened whipped cream or crème fraîche and cracked chocolate-covered espresso beans for serving**

1 Preheat the oven to 425°F and position a rack in the center. Butter and flour an 8-inch springform pan and dust with cocoa, tapping out the excess.

2 In a large, heavy saucepan, combine the chocolate, butter, and espresso and stir over low heat until melted. Scrape into a bowl and, using a whisk, stir in the vanilla and ½ cup of the granulated sugar. Beat in the egg yolks, one at a time, then beat in the flour.

3 In a clean bowl and using clean beaters, beat the egg whites on high speed until they hold soft peaks. Gradually add the remaining 2 tablespoons granulated sugar and beat until silky and smooth, 1 minute longer. Beat one quarter of the whites into the chocolate batter, then, using a rubber spatula, fold in the remaining whites. Scrape the batter into the prepared pan and turn the oven temperature down to 350°F. Bake for about 25 minutes or until a toothpick inserted in the center comes out clean. Transfer the pan to a rack and let cool for 30 minutes. Remove the pan ring and let cool completely.

4 Dust the top with confectioners' sugar and serve with the sweetened whipped cream or crème fraîche and the chocolate espresso beans.

Season 2, Episode 24

MANNY, CARRYING A BASEBALL GLOVE:

Hey, Cam.

CAM:

Oh, hey, Manny.

MANNY:

Mom, is Jay still here?

GLORIA:

No, he just left.

MANNY:

Shoot!

CAM:

Why? What's up, pal?

MANNY:

I'm going over to a friend's house where I may have to use this thing. I've only used it once and that was to take a torte out of the oven.

Season 3, Episode 3

GLORIA, HOLDING A
CHEWED-UP SHOE:

It's ruined. Stella did this.
She chew on my shoe.
You have to discipline
that stupid dog.

JAY:

I discipline her all the time.

GLORIA:

Oh, really? How? By buying
her little cupcakes?

JAY:

They're not real cupcakes.
They're doggie treats in the
form of cupcakes.

GLORIA:

Yeah. You should've told that
to Manny before he ate one.

stella's | peanut butter *and* bacon pupcakes

*Makes about 24 (3-inch) dog biscuits**

1 cup creamy natural peanut butter

¾ cup unsalted chicken broth

¼ cup unsweetened applesauce

2 cups whole-wheat flour

2 teaspoons baking powder

⅓ cup quick-cooking oats

¼ cup chopped cooked bacon (about 6 slices)

1 Preheat the oven to 325°F. Line two baking sheets with parchment paper.

2 In a large bowl, combine the peanut butter, broth, and applesauce; stir until smooth. In another bowl, combine all the remaining ingredients, stirring to combine evenly. Add the dry ingredients to the wet ingredients in batches, stirring well between additions until thoroughly incorporated. Turn the dough out onto a work surface and knead a few times. Roll out to ¼-inch thickness and cut with a cupcake-shaped cookie cutter.

3 Place the cut dough ½ inch apart on the prepared baking sheets. Bake for 12 minutes, then gently turn the cookies over and bake for an additional 12 minutes, then turn again and bake for 2 minutes (this will make them good and crisp).

4 Let cool completely before serving, one at a time. Store in a zip-top plastic bag in the refrigerator for up to 2 weeks.

* *These are not for humans!*

jay's | cherries jubilee

Serves 4

⅓ **cup red currant jelly**

1 (16-ounce) can pitted Bing cherries, drained

¼ **cup brandy**

Vanilla ice cream

1 Melt the jelly in a flat skillet; add the cherries. Cook over medium heat until bubbly; set aside and keep warm.

2 Put the brandy in a small long-handled pan; heat just until warm. Pour the brandy over the cherries and ignite with a long match. Baste the cherries with the sauce until the flames die down. Serve immediately over the ice cream.

Season 4, Episode 11

GLORIA:

Jay, you should go back and spend time with your family.

JAY:

I can't leave you alone on New Year's Eve. Even though everyone's waiting for me to come back.

GLORIA:

Oh, that's so sweet.

JAY:

I just hope I don't hold up the lighting of the cherries jubilee.

must love dogs

Everyone loves dogs, but sometimes Jay Pritchett's family wonders if he loves his French bulldog, Stella, more than he loves his people. He cuddles her. He coddles her. And he has a much easier time expressing affection for her than he ever has with his wife and kids. Does your family ever wonder if you love your dog best too? If you answer yes to most of the questions below, they just might!

○ yes ○ no — Would you rather take your dog to a Bark Mitzvah than take your wife to a party with her friends?

○ yes ○ no — If your dog and your wife both fall into the swimming pool, do you hand your dog a towel to dry off first?

○ yes ○ no — When your wife tells you your dog and your son need to spend a week apart to test your son's allergies, is your first thought: "I don't want to go a whole week without seeing my son"?

○ yes ○ no — Do you ever shout out, "Oh, baby!" when you're dreaming about your dog?

○ yes ○ no — Was it easier for you to drop off your son at sports camp than it was to drop off your dog with a dogsitter for a week?

○ yes ○ no — Do you cuddle more with your dog than you do with your wife?

○ yes ○ no — Do you think it's crazy to leave work early to prepare a meal for your family, but perfectly normal to leave work early to cook a steak dinner for your dog?

○ yes ○ no — When you say, "I figure, if she looks beautiful, she'll feel beautiful," are you talking about buying your dog a decorative show collar, and not about buying your wife jewelry?

○ yes ○ no — Are you more impressed that your dog admires her own reflection in hubcaps than you are that your son does well on tests at school?

○ yes ○ no — When you ask, "How's my little angel?" in a room with your whole family, do your kids know you're talking about your dog and not about them?

○ yes ○ no — Would you rather use your phone to record a video of your dog doing something cute than FaceTime with your kids?

MANNY:

The universe is cold and loveless.

CAM:

Uh-oh, bad Valentine's Day?

MANNY:

I went for the gold—Fiona Gunderson. I poured my heart and soul into a poem and left it on her desk. I even burned the edges to make it look fancy.

CAM:

And she didn't like it?

MANNY:

Oh, she loved it. But this kid Durkas told her he wrote it.

manny's | tiramisu

Serves 12

¼ cup brandy

2 tablespoons plus 1 teaspoon instant espresso granules

1 (3-ounce) package cakelike ladyfingers, split in half horizontally

1 cup sugar

4 large egg whites

1 (8.8-ounce) carton mascarpone cheese

1 cup plain fat-free yogurt

¼ cup sweet Marsala wine

1½ teaspoons unsweetened cocoa

1 Combine the brandy, ¼ cup water, and 2 tablespoons of the espresso granules; stir well. Place 2 ladyfinger halves in the bottom of each of 12 (4-ounce) coffee cups. Brush the brandy mixture evenly over the ladyfingers. Set aside.

2 Add water to a large saucepan to a depth of 1 inch; bring to a simmer over medium heat. Reduce the heat to medium-low. Combine the sugar and egg whites in a large metal bowl large enough to sit on top of but not in the saucepan. Place the bowl over the saucepan of simmering water; cook the egg-white mixture for 20 minutes or until a thermometer registers 160°F, stirring constantly. Remove the bowl from the saucepan; beat the egg mixture with an electric mixer at high speed for 8 minutes or until stiff peaks form.

3 Beat the mascarpone, yogurt, and wine in a large bowl on medium speed until blended and smooth. Gently fold in the egg-white mixture. Divide the mixture evenly among the coffee cups lined with ladyfingers. Sift the cocoa and the remaining 1 teaspoon espresso granules evenly over the tops of the desserts. Cover and chill in the refrigerator for at least 8 hours. Serve cold.

gloria's | dulce de leche flan

Serves 8

1 (14-ounce) can sweetened
   condensed milk

Cooking spray

½ cup sugar

2 cups milk

3 large eggs

2 large egg
   whites

½ teaspoon
   vanilla
   extract

1 Preheat the oven to 425°F.

2 Pour the sweetened condensed milk into a 1-quart baking
   dish; cover and place in a broiler pan. Add hot water to
   the pan to a depth of 1 inch. Bake for 45 minutes or until
   the milk is thick and caramel-colored. Remove the dish
   from the pan; uncover and let cool to room temperature.

3 Reduce the oven temperature to 325°F. Coat a 9-inch round cake pan with
   cooking spray.

4 Combine the sugar and ¼ cup water in a small, heavy saucepan and cook
   over medium-high heat until the sugar dissolves, stirring frequently. Continue cooking, stirring constantly, for 5 minutes or until golden. Immediately
   pour the caramel into the prepared cake pan, tipping the pan quickly to coat
   the bottom of the pan with the caramel.

5 Spoon the condensed milk into a large bowl. Add the milk, whole eggs,
   egg whites, and vanilla; stir with a whisk until well blended. Strain the milk
   mixture through a fine sieve into the prepared pan over the caramel and
   discard the solids. Place the cake pan in the bottom of the broiler pan; add
   hot water to the pan to a depth of 1 inch. Bake for 40 minutes or until a knife
   inserted in the center comes out clean.

6 Remove from the oven and let the flan cool to room temperature in the
   water bath. Remove the cake pan from the water bath, cover, and chill in
   the refrigerator for at least 3 hours or overnight. Loosen the edges of the
   flan with a knife or rubber spatula. Place a plate, upside down, on top of the
   cake pan; invert the flan onto the plate. Drizzle any remaining caramelized
   syrup over the flan and serve cold.

Season 2, Episode 17

JAY:

Listen, I've been thinking.
When I go, I want you to
know, it's okay if you
marry someone else.

GLORIA:

I know.

JAY:

'Cause I want you to
be happy.

GLORIA:

I'll be happy.

JAY:

You're driving me crazy
on purpose, right?

Season 4, Episode 8

MANNY:

No girl's ever smiled at me like that. Luke, we have to go to that bar mitzvah.

LUKE:

Why?

MANNY:

There was a connection. I know this sounds crazy. But I feel like my whole life has led to this moment.

LUKE:

You made a very similar speech to get my mom to stop for those churros.

manny's | churros *with* hot chocolate

Makes about 36 (5-inch) churros

FOR THE CHURROS:

½ cup (1 stick) unsalted butter

Kosher salt

1 cup all-purpose flour

4 large eggs

1 quart vegetable oil

1 cup sugar

2 tablespoons ground cinnamon

FOR THE HOT CHOCOLATE:

8 ounces bittersweet chocolate (60% to 72%), chopped

1½ cups heavy cream

Pinch of kosher salt

1　Make the churros: In a medium saucepan, bring 1 cup water to a boil. Add the butter and ½ teaspoon salt and cook over medium heat just until the butter is melted. Add the flour all at once and cook, stirring vigorously with a wooden spoon, until the dough comes together and forms a cohesive mass, 1 to 2 minutes. Remove from the heat and let sit for 2 to 3 minutes. Off the heat, using a handheld electric mixer on medium speed, beat the flour mixture for 1 minute. On medium speed, beat in the eggs, one at a time, until combined and a sticky dough forms.

2　Heat the oil in a large saucepan to 375°F. Line a large baking sheet with a wire rack, and cover the rack with paper towels.

3　In a large pie plate, combine the sugar with the cinnamon and a pinch of salt. Put the dough in a large pastry bag fitted with a large star tip. Working quickly, holding the bag in one hand and a small table knife in the other, squeeze 5-inch lengths of the dough into the hot oil, cutting them off with the knife. Fry no more than 8 at a time, as the churros expand a bit as they cook. Cook over medium-high heat, turning once or twice, until deeply browned, about 5 minutes. Drain on paper towels for a minute, then toss in the cinnamon sugar. Transfer to a platter and repeat with the remaining dough.

4　Make the hot chocolate: Put the chocolate in a heat-proof bowl. Heat the cream in a small saucepan until bubbles appear around the edges and it's steaming. Pour the hot cream over the chocolate and let sit for 2 minutes. Add the salt and whisk until smooth. Pour the chocolate into demitasse cups or small ramekins and serve with the warm churros.

DRINKS

phil's | killer margs

Serves 12

¾ cup sugar

1¾ cups tequila

1 cup fresh lime juice (from about 5 limes)

½ cup orange-flavored liqueur

Lime wedges (optional)

Kosher salt (optional)

6 cups crushed ice

1 Combine 1¾ cups water and the sugar in a small saucepan. Bring to a boil; boil for 3 minutes, stirring until the sugar is dissolved. Remove from the heat. Place the pan in a large ice-filled bowl until the syrup cools to room temperature (about 10 minutes), stirring occasionally.

2 Combine the syrup, tequila, lime juice, and liqueur in a pitcher. If desired, rub a lime wedge around the rims of 12 margarita glasses and dip the rims in the salt. Place ½ cup crushed ice in each glass. Pour the margarita mixture evenly over the ice. Garnish with lime wedges, if desired, and serve immediately.

Season 3, Episode 14

PHIL:

[He] got divorced, and his whole life opened up. Guy's livin' the dream.

(CLAIRE GLARES AT HIM)

His dream. Not my dream. I'm living my dream. You're my dream.

CLAIRE:

You can stop.

Season 2, Episode 1

KELLY:

Ooh, you know what you should do? Put a pinch of salt in the chocolate milk. It really brings out the flavor.

GLORIA:

Salt is for the popcorn.

MANNY:

That sounds good.

GLORIA, TO MANNY:

You wouldn't like it.

Season 4, Episode 11

MANNY:

Can I offer you a Piña Delgado? It's my own concoction.

JOYCE:

What's in it?

MANNY:

Let's just say it's cool. It's sweet. And it's not afraid to embrace its own whimsy.

manny's | girlfriend's salted chocolate milk

Makes 1 cup chocolate concentrate; serves 4 or 5

¼ cup unsweetened cocoa powder

1 cup sugar

1 cup boiling water

¼ cup light corn syrup

Milk

Kosher salt

1 In a small saucepan, combine the cocoa powder, sugar, boiling water, and corn syrup and bring to a boil. Simmer over low heat until slightly thickened and reduced to 1 cup, about 10 minutes. Pour into a heat-proof bowl and let cool completely.

2 Pour the milk into tall glasses. Add a few tablespoons of the chocolate syrup to each and stir until combined. Add a pinch of salt and serve right away.

manny's | piña delgado

Serves 4

1 ripe banana, peeled and cut into 1-inch pieces

2 teaspoons fresh lemon juice

1 mango, peeled, pitted, and cut into ½-inch pieces

1½ cups pineapple-orange juice, chilled

1 cup vanilla nonfat frozen yogurt

1 teaspoon coconut extract

1 Toss the banana with the lemon juice in a small bowl. Transfer the banana to a baking sheet, reserving the lemon juice; freeze until solid.

2 Put the banana, reserved lemon juice, mango, pineapple-orange juice, frozen yogurt, and coconut extract in a blender and blend until smooth. Pour into chilled glasses and serve immediately.

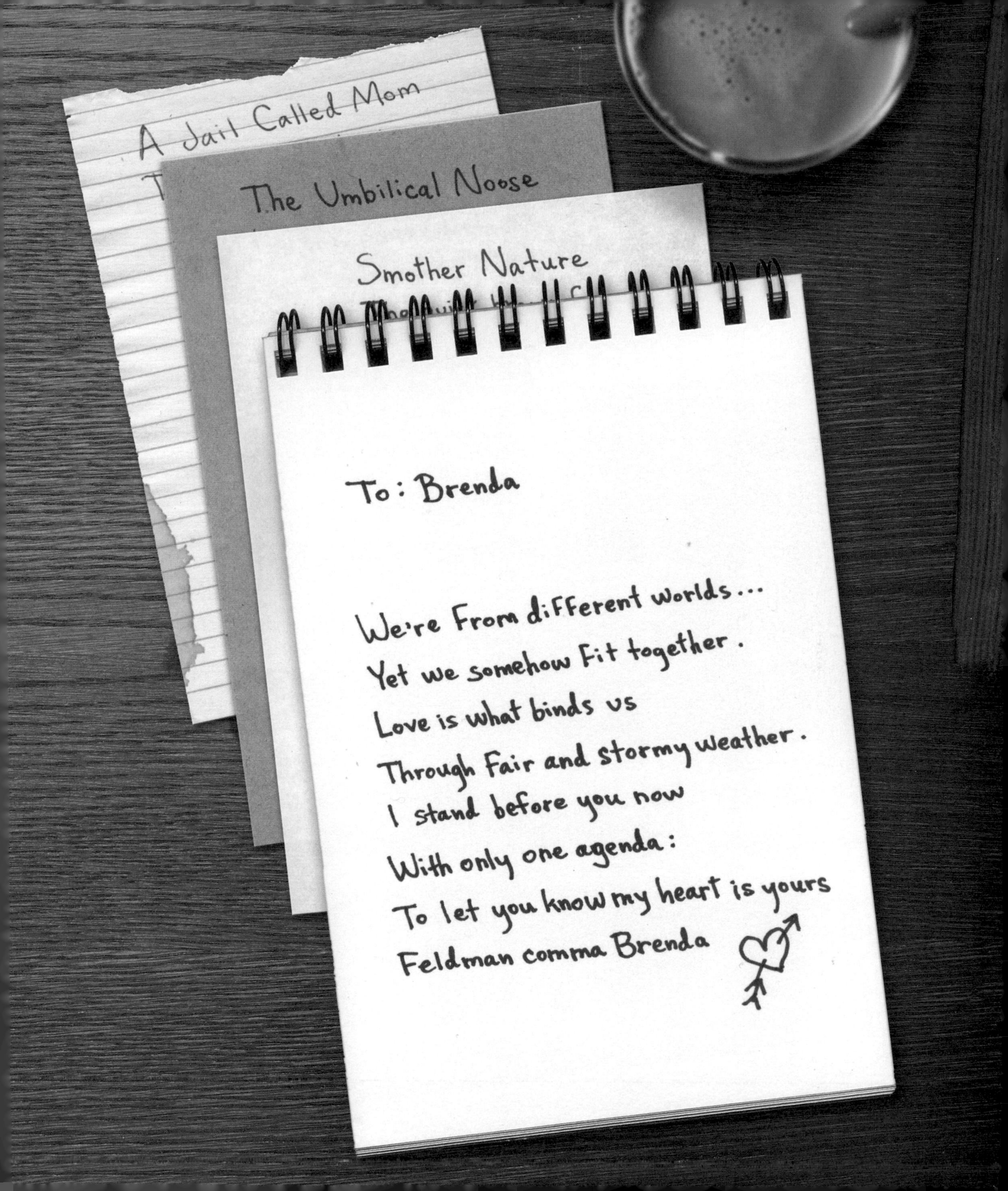

A Jail Called Mom

The Umbilical Noose

Smother Nature

To: Brenda

We're from different worlds...
Yet we somehow fit together.
Love is what binds us
Through fair and stormy weather.
I stand before you now
With only one agenda:
To let you know my heart is yours
Feldman comma Brenda

GLORIA:

So, Lily, tell me more about this Patrick.

LILY:

He likes the swings, he sits by the flag, and he can count to a hundred.

GLORIA:

He sounds like the whole package. Then what is the problem?

LILY:

He doesn't notice me.

GLORIA:

So then make him notice you. You don't want to wake up one morning as a lonely nine-year-old, wondering where all the time went.

lily's | sparkling strawberry lemonade

Serves 10

1 (12-ounce) package frozen unsweetened strawberries, thawed

2 (12-ounce) cans frozen pink lemonade concentrate, thawed and undiluted

4 cups berry-flavored sparkling water, chilled

Lemon slices (optional)

1 Blend the strawberries in a blender until smooth, stopping once to scrape down the sides. Pour the strawberry puree through a fine sieve into a large freezer-proof container, discarding the pulp and seeds. Add the lemonade and 2 cups water; stir well. Cover and freeze for 4 hours or until slushy.

2 To serve, transfer the lemonade mixture to a large pitcher or a small punch bowl. Stir in the sparkling water and serve immediately. Garnish with the lemon slices, if desired.

CLAIRE, REFERRING TO THE WAITER:
Well, that Brian sure is a cutie, huh?

PHIL:
I'd kill to have those lips. I mean on me. I mean I want his lips on my mouth.

HALEY:
Uh, can we just cut to the chase?

PHIL:
He's got great lips.

HALEY:
No, no, no. What are we doing here? What is this about?

CLAIRE:
Nothing! We just wanted to have a fun night out with our daughter.

PHIL:
Yeah! Just think of us as your friends.

CLAIRE:
Yeah!

HALEY:
I don't have 45-year-old friends.

CLAIRE:
Well, you don't have 45-year-old parents yet, either, honey, so calm down.

claire *and* phil's | basil-infused mojitos

Serves 12

3 cups white rum

2¼ cups fresh lime juice

2 cups Basil-Infused Simple Syrup, or more to taste (recipe follows)

½ teaspoon West Indian orange bitters

4 cups club soda or sparkling water

Fresh basil leaves

Lime twists

1 In a large pitcher, combine the rum, lime juice, simple syrup, and bitters. Chill for at least 2 hours or up to 1 day.

2 To make each drink, fill an old-fashioned glass with ice and pour in about ⅔ cup of the rum mixture. Top with ⅓ cup club soda. Garnish with basil leaves and a lime twist. Serve immediately.

NOTE: When you're mixing these mojitos for a big family gathering, it's best to make a large batch of the basil simple syrup and go ahead and mix it with the rum, lime juice, and bitters in a pitcher. That way you can have it all ready in advance and just top off each drink with club soda, rather than making each drink individually.

basil-infused simple syrup

Makes about 2¼ cups

1½ cups sugar

2 (1-ounce) packages fresh basil leaves

1 Combine the sugar and 1½ cups water in a small saucepan. Bring to a boil over medium-high heat; cook, stirring occasionally, for 5 minutes or until the sugar is dissolved. Remove from the heat. Stir in the basil. Let steep for 1 hour.

2 Pour the syrup through a fine-mesh sieve into a glass measuring cup, pressing the basil with the back of a spoon. Discard the basil. Cover and chill until ready to use; store in the refrigerator for up to 1 week.

claire's | swampwater punch

Serves 15 to 20

1 **(12-ounce) can frozen orange juice concentrate, partially thawed**

1 **quart white grape juice**

5 **drops green food coloring**

Gummy worms or gummy frogs

1 **(2-liter) bottle lemon-lime soda**

1 Combine the juices, 1½ cups water, and the food coloring in a large pitcher; chill in the refrigerator.

2 Arrange the gummy worms or frogs in the bottom of a 5-cup ring mold. Fill the mold with water; freeze until solid, 8 hours to overnight.

3 At serving time, turn out the ice ring and place it in a punch bowl. Pour the chilled juice mixture into the punch bowl; slowly pour in the soda. Serve immediately.

dede's | horny colombian cocktails

Serves 1

¼ **cup añejo dark rum**

2 **tablespoons chilled pineapple juice**

2 **tablespoons chilled mango juice**

2 **teaspoons fresh lime juice**

4 **dashes rhubarb bitters**

1 **teaspoon grenadine**

Pineapple wedges

1 Put ice in a cocktail shaker. Add the rum, pineapple juice, mango juice, lime juice, and bitters. Cover with the lid; shake vigorously until thoroughly chilled (about 30 seconds). Strain the mixture into a chilled martini glass. Float the grenadine on top. Garnish with a pineapple wedge or two and serve immediately.

Season 6, Episode 6

PHIL, AFTER CLAIRE COMES HOME UNEXPECTEDLY:

What are you even doing here? Shouldn't you be at work?

CLAIRE:

That obnoxious Ronnie was worried that I wouldn't be able to handle his decorations, 'cause he's trying to win this "scariest house on the street" contest, and I was like, "Not only can I handle your decorations. I'm gonna win that contest." So welcome to the Insane Asylum from Hell.

PHIL:

That's what it feels like.

Season 1, Episode 4

CLAIRE:

My mom started drinking these cocktails called "Horny Colombians" with some of Gloria's uncles, whom apparently the drink was named after.

PHIL:

Oh, come on, they were funny.

CLAIRE:

They kept patting my butt.

PHIL:

Somebody's full of herself.

modern family secrets

Like most families, the Dunphy-Tucker-Pritchett-Delgados have some skeletons in the closet. From a secret shooting habit and a hidden puppeteer past to a Facebook alias and a fake job, this clan is not afraid to stretch the truth and shift the blame. Here are ten of their biggest secrets and lies (a couple of which are still under the rug).

10

Red Juice Box Blues

When Lily's strawberry juice box exploded on a neighbor's $50,000 rug, Cam and Mitchell blamed it on the neighbor's kid. It turned out that he was allergic to strawberries and would have needed a special injection if he had actually sipped any of the juice. Cam and Mitchell went as far as holding him down so his mom could give him the emergency shot, before confessing that the juice box was Lily's.

9

The NyQuil Incident

Left with the kids for the day, Phil accidentally gave Alex the wrong medicine, which left her groggy and disoriented. He initially tried to convince Claire that Alex was just going through a growth spurt, but eventually he confessed that he unwittingly drugged her with nighttime allergy medicine.

8

Uncle Grumpy

When Luke and Manny discovered an old suitcase in the attic, Gloria initially refused to let them open it. Luke assumed it was a human head, and he was sort of right. Gloria gave in and unpacked Uncle Grumpy, the puppet she used for her ventriloquism act in her beauty pageant days.

7

Ghostwriting Chuck Stone

Jay swore to Gloria that he had the capacity to write a great spy novel, but he couldn't write a single page. Meantime, Manny banged out a full book about a character named Chuck Stone—"They taught him how to kill, but he never learned to love!"—and gave Jay credit. When a suspicious Gloria pointed out that Stone couldn't have had a cell phone because his story took place in the 1960s, Manny confessed his authorship.

6

Brody Kendall

While logged into her Brody Kendall Facebook account—a fake profile she created to spy on her kids—Claire saw that Haley had updated her relationship status to "Married" and became convinced that Haley had run off to Las Vegas to marry Andy. Fortunately for everyone, Haley's update was a joke. She didn't marry Andy; she "married" a cronut.

5

The Bad Seed

Despite the fact that Joe couldn't walk at the time, Lily blamed the baby for pulling Gloria's purse off the table and breaking her phone. She also accused him of knocking over a bottle of baby powder and leaving footprints all over the floor. Jay and Gloria asked her to prove that Joe would walk for her and, miraculously, he did. In a subsequent camera confessional, Lily announced her intention to "blame everything on him until he learns how to talk."

4

Not-So-Cool Hand Luke

When Manny got invited to a sophomore's pool party and Luke didn't, Manny kept it a secret to spare Luke's feelings. Luke found out anyway and confessed that life was easier when Manny was ostrich-size. "You know, like a freaky outsider? The way an ostrich feels around regular birds."

3

Save the Date

When Cam expressed his excitement that no one had RSVP'd "no" to the benefit he'd spent months planning, Mitchell suddenly realized that he'd never mailed the invitations. Mitchell tried to round up guests at the last minute, even going as far as handing out flyers at the mall, but he couldn't hide his mistake from Cam. In the end, though, Mitchell filled every seat in the house.

2

The Great Waitress Hoax

Phil and Claire thought Haley was waitressing to save up for a car, but Alex realized that she was scamming her parents. Alex organized a family outing to the restaurant in an attempt to blow her sister's cover, but her plan was foiled when Claire and Phil spent the entire dinner arguing about wedge salad, and Haley used the opportunity to stage her own firing.

1

Ready, Aim, Namaste

Gloria tried to join Claire for yoga class, but Claire blew her off so many times that Gloria finally called her out on it. That's when Claire confessed that "yoga" was actually her code name for the shooting range, where she goes regularly to decompress.

MENUS

Every family has its own traditions. For the Dunphys, Halloween is the most anticipated event of the year—it's just a question of whether the theme is blood and guts or candy and cuteness. The Tucker-Pritchetts love any excuse for a good party, but game night is a recurring favorite. And the Pritchett-Delgados are always eager to have everyone over for a barbecue—even if they're really only there for the pool. Here are some favorite special-occasion menus from the entire crew, all comprised from the recipes in this book.

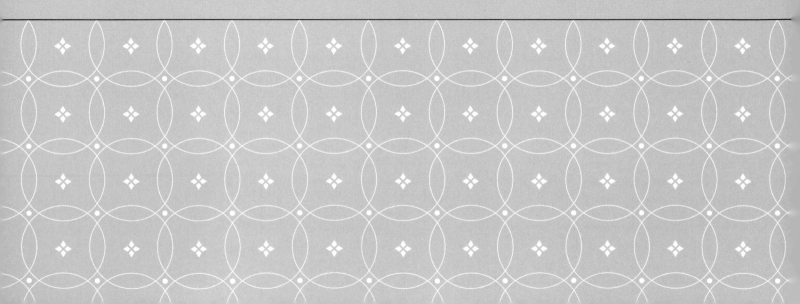

menus

*What?! Well, whose room
is this then?*

—PHIL

*What if I was all, "Knock, knock." And
they were like, "Who's there?" And I was
all, "Someone who doesn't want to see their
parents doing it, that's why we knocked."*

—PHIL

CLIVE AND JULIANA'S
DATE NIGHT DINNER

ANNIVERSARY BREAKFAST
IN BED

CLAIRE'S ARUGULA SALAD
with Prosciutto *and* Pears   *page 84*

PHIL'S MULTIGRAIN
MALT WAFFLES   *page 24*

PHIL'S HONEY-ROASTED
CORNISH HEN   *page 181*

ALEX'S FRESH FRUIT SALAD
with Lime-Ginger Syrup   *page 28*

CLAIRE'S GREEN BEANS
with Toasted Almonds *and* Lemon   *page 122*

CLAIRE'S WHITE BEAN
and TOMATO SALAD   *page 83*

CLAIRE *and* PHIL'S CHERRY
CLAFOUTI   *page 216*

m e n u s

Happy Valentine's Day! It's the one time of the year when the world tries to be as romantic as I am all the time. Good luck, world.

—MANNY

You win an Oscar.
You buy a Golden Globe.

—CAM

VALENTINE'S DAY SWEEP HER OFF HER FEAST

OSCAR PARTY

MANNY'S
CHARCUTERIE PLATE   *page 65*

CLAIRE *and* PHIL'S
BASIL-INFUSED
MOJITOS   *page 234*

MANNY'S
CHOCOLATE TORTE   *page 217*

CAM *and* MITCHELL'S
BUTTERNUT SQUASH BISQUE
(serve in shot glasses)   *page 96*

MANNY'S
GIRLFRIEND'S SALTED
CHOCOLATE MILK   *page 230*

CAM'S ROASTED PEPPER
and BEEF CROSTINI   *page 53*

MITCHELL'S SMOKED
SALMON CANAPÉS   *page 74*

m e n u s

It's true, Jay. I cheated.
I cheat a little bit every time that we
come to play game night.

—GLORIA

I think the whole idea of needing a
prince to come along and make you happy
sends the wrong message, Mitchell. I really do.

—CAM

FAMILY GAME NIGHT

MITCHELL'S SO-CAL
TOMATILLO-AVOCADO DIP   *page 51*

GLORIA'S CARNITAS
AL DIABLO   *page 160*

CAM'S COFFEE-FROSTED
BROWNIES   *page 196*

JAY'S MOVIE NIGHT CINNAMON-
SUGAR POPCORN   *page 50*

PRINCESS BIRTHDAY PARTY

LILY'S POT STICKERS   *page 79*

LILY'S PINEAPPLE CAKE   *page 208*

LILY'S SPARKLING STRAWBERRY
LEMONADE   *page 232*

menus

Electric rotisserie!
If God wants a hamburger, this is
what She cooks it on.

—PHIL

The leading cause of death
among Colombian women is when
their sons get married.

—GLORIA

FOURTH OF JULY BARBECUE POTLUCK

COLOMBIAN INDEPENDENCE DAY FIESTA

*This summer, all the Dunphys
are just clicking.*

—PHIL

*Pepper has done the impossible—
he's made two gay men hate brunch.*

—MITCHELL

THE PERFECT
SUMMER DINNER

CLAIRE'S HONEY-PEPPERED
GOAT CHEESE

with Fig Balsamic Drizzle   *page 54*

PHIL'S LAMB CHOPS
with Minted Yogurt   *page 148*

LUKE'S RHUBARB PIE   *page 214*

SUNDAY FUNDAY BRUNCH

CAM'S GRANDMOTHER'S
HOUSEKEEPER DELILAH'S
BISCUITS *and* GRAVY   *page 39*

MITCHELL'S VEGETABLE-
GRUYÈRE QUICHE   *page 36*

MITCHELL'S ROSEMARY-INFUSED
GRAPEFRUIT COMPOTE   *page 212*

menus

We should just put out a bowl of candy and have a cocktail, right?

—CLAIRE

How am I supposed to feed eleven people with this pigeon?!

—PHIL

HALLOWEEN SPOOKTACULAR

A DUNPHY THANKSGIVING

Everything fun is your dad.
Second Christmas, Italian accent night.

—CLAIRE

You better drink that smoothie.
We're going on a run!

—ANDY

ITALIAN ACCENT NIGHT

CLAIRE'S WHITE BEAN *and*
TOMATO SALAD   *page 83*

CLAIRE'S
PESTO SHRIMP PASTA   *page 168*

MANNY'S TIRAMISU   *page 222*

HEALTH KICK WITH
ANDY THE MANNY

JOE'S FRUIT-YOGURT POPS   *page 48*

ANDY'S BLUEBERRY-
POMEGRANATE SMOOTHIE   *page 29*

ANDY'S
FLAXSEED MUFFINS   *page 193*

ANDY'S
RED QUINOA SALAD   *page 89*

ANDY'S PARTLY EGG-WHITE
MEDITERRANEAN-STYLE
FRITTATA   *page 138*

modernfamily™

EPISODE GUIDE

If you've purchased this cookbook, it's likely you're already a *Modern Family* fan, but chances are that you've missed an episode here or there. The guide on the following pages isn't meant to be comprehensive, but it does offer a nice summary of each episode's major events. Think of it as a quick refresher course on all the wacky antics of the Dunphy-Tucker-Pritchett-Delgado clan.

episode 1

ep 1   Pilot

Phil schedules time to shoot Luke; Manny woos an older girl; Cam and Mitchell bring home "the little pot sticker."

ep 2   The Bicycle Thief

Phil teaches Luke a valuable lesson in bike ownership and larceny, while Jay spends quality time with Manny, and Cam and Mitchell endure a toddler play class.

episode 4

ep 3   Come Fly with Me

Jay and Phil try to take their relationship to the next level, as Phil has apparently done with Dylan. Claire makes chocolate chip cookies, in which the secret ingredient is caring.

ep 4   The Incident

A bird crashes into a window, an ancient harbinger of bad things to come. Mitchell and Claire's mom shows up for a surprise visit, attempting to make amends.

ep 5   Coal Digger

Luke and Manny get into a schoolyard brawl that gives new meaning to the phrase "Say 'uncle.'" At a family barbecue, Claire and Gloria square off over dueling pies.

ep 6   Run for Your Wife

Manny debates wearing a Colombian poncho to school. Cam expertly pronounces the Vietnamese word pho, making a tense emergency pediatrician visit even more awkward.

ep 7   En Garde

Jay's pride in Manny's fencing success brings out latent feelings of rejection in Jay's biological children. Phil encourages Luke to "pursue excellence," with mixed results.

ep 8   Great Expectations

Claire and Phil celebrate their anniversary with Cornish hens and imbalanced gift-giving. The lead guitarist (actually bass player) of Spandau Ballet makes an appearance. Jay has the kids over for Sloppy Jay's.

ep 9   Fizbo

Phil and Claire plan the ultimate birthday party for Luke. Fizbo's aggressive and surprisingly masculine side takes Mitchell aback.

ep 10   Undeck the Halls

A cigarette-size hole has been burned into the Dunphy couch, and Phil and Claire threaten to take away Christmas unless someone confesses. Gloria brings a little Colombia to the holiday celebrations with her traditional buñuelos.

ep 11   Up All Night

Manny's father, Javier, shows up. Mitchell and Cam try to figure out their respective parenting roles.

ep 12   Not in My House

Manny has a romantic tomato soup and grilled cheese lunch date. Claire finds a picture of a naked woman on a tractor on her computer and assumes it's Luke's, but Phil is the real guilty party.

ep 13   Fifteen Percent

When Cam runs into Jay and his tough-guy pals, extreme awkwardness occurs. Manny has a blind date. Technology: 0; Claire: 1.

ep 14   Moon Landing

Claire misses having a "real" job. Jay actually acknowledges that Mitchell is an attorney and asks him for legal help.

ep 15   My Funky Valentine

Claire and Phil try role-playing; Jay takes Gloria to a comedy show where the comedian "doesn't do jokes"; Cam and Mitchell play cupid for Manny.

ep 16   Fears

Luke helps Phil overcome his fear of the crawlspace, while Manny and Lily's dads work on fears of their own.

ep 17   Truth Be Told

Jay has trouble fessing up to Manny about a tragic accident. Mitchell feels like he's missing out on Lily's milestones.

ep 18   Starry Night

Gloria takes Cam to her favorite hole-in-the-wall. Claire makes forty bake-sale cupcakes.

ep 19   Game Changer

Phil's birthday starts out on a high note, but quickly goes downhill. Jay instructs Manny in chess.

ep 20   Benched

Phil and Jay have differing approaches to steak cooking and basketball coaching. Cam accompanies Mitchell to an important work-social gathering.

ep 21   Travels with Scout

Phil's dad shows up unexpectedly in an RV—with a special friend. Cam joins a band.

episode 14

ep 22   Airport 2010

Jay thinks he's embarking on an intimate birthday getaway to Hawaii with Gloria and a stack of Robert Ludlum novels. He's in for a surprise.

ep 23   Hawaii

Everyone has their own idea of what the perfect Hawaiian vacation entails.

ep 24   Family Portrait

Claire micromanages a family portrait. Cam scores a gig as a wedding singer, but Mitchell sits out the wedding so he doesn't have to make small talk.

episode 24

season two

ep 1   The Old Wagon
Gloria and Manny's new girlfriend face off over chocolate milk and empanadas. Mitchell and Cam construct a play castle for Lily.

ep 2   The Kiss
To honor her late grandmother, Gloria cooks traditional Colombian meals.

ep 3   Earthquake
A natural disaster of minor proportions gives Mitchell and Cam an excuse to opt out of Pepper's brunch.

ep 4   Strangers on a Treadmill
Phil prepares for a presentation at the mother of all residential real estate banquets, the SCARB.

episode 9

ep 5   Unplugged
The Dunphys challenge one another to go without devices.

ep 6   Halloween
What could go wrong in Claire and Phil's House of Horrors?

episode 20

ep 7   Chirp
Mitchell has reservations about Lily becoming a child actress; Cam has none. Phil's business takes a downturn.

ep 8   Manny Get Your Gun
An inappropriate birthday present sends Manny into a tailspin. Mitchell cheats on Cam with choreography.

ep 9   Mother Tucker
Cam's mother gets too close for comfort. Haley and Dylan break up, and Phil steps in to help ease Dylan's pain.

ep 10   Dance Dance Revelation
Claire and Gloria co-chair the school dance planning committee. Phil and Jay try to exhibit maturity to Luke and Manny, each failing spectacularly. Lily is a biter.

episode 2

ep 11   Slow Down Your Neighbors
A handsome stranger appears in Cam and Mitchell's hot tub. Meanwhile, Claire takes on an aggressive driver in the neighborhood.

ep 12   Our Children, Ourselves
Phil and Claire, in an attempt to be more intellectual, go to see a foreign film. Mitchell runs into an old flame—a female old flame, with a redheaded son.

ep 13   Caught in the Act
The Dunphy kids serve their parents an anniversary breakfast in bed, and see something they wish they hadn't. Mitchell and Cam try to finagle a reservation at the hot new restaurant in town.

ep 14   Bixby's Back
Juliana makes an unexpected appearance on Valentine's Day. Cam and Mitchell order extra tiramisu.

ep 15   Princess Party
Psycho, scary, drunk: things that Claire can get when her mother comes to visit.

ep 16   Regrets Only
Claire, after a blowout fight with Phil about a wedge salad, takes comfort in a dirty habit. Cam throws a benefit party.

ep 17   Two Monkeys and a Panda
Phil sneaks a spa day and gets some good advice. Mitchell discovers that the new spinach is kale.

ep 18   Boys' Night
Manny and Jay are reluctant to try new things. Phil and Claire meet Luke's new friend, Walt, the crotchety old man next door.

ep 19   The Musical Man
Phil's new advertisement, plastered on the family SUV, features Haley and Claire—and a questionable slogan. Cam goes overboard directing the school musical.

ep 20   Someone to Watch Over Lily
Whom will Mitchell and Cam choose as guardians for Lily should tragedy strike them both?

ep 21   Mother's Day
A pleasant Mother's Day hike in the mountains turns dramatic. Jay shows some vulnerability over a pot of tomato sauce and an old memory.

episode 13

ep 22   Good Cop Bad Dog
The natural order is disrupted when Claire decides to become the "fun" parent, leaving Phil to be the enforcer.

ep 23   See You Next Fall
Alex is graduating from middle school, but will her parents make it to the ceremony to see her give the commencement speech?

ep 24   The One That Got Away
Claire and Mitchell hash out some issues while re-creating an old photograph of them as kids for Jay's birthday.

episode 1

ep 1 Dude Ranch

The family vacations in Wyoming, and Phil is on a mission to impress Jay with his cowboy skills.

ep 2 When Good Kids Go Bad

Mitchell and Cam have an announcement to make to the family, but first they need to get Lily on board with sharing her dads with a baby brother. Luke manipulates his sisters to get the attic bedroom.

ep 3 Phil on a Wire

Cam starts a juice fast, and Mitchell is supportive. Haley and Alex find themselves in the same math class. Stella drives a wedge between Gloria and Jay.

ep 4 Door to Door

Jay instructs Manny in the art of the hard sell. Claire finds a cause and dives into hyperlocal politics.

ep 5 Hit and Run

Claire considers running for city council. Cam and Mitchell are the victims of a hit-and-run accident.

ep 6 Go Bullfrogs!

Haley goes on a college visit with Phil. Cam and Mitchell take Claire for a much-needed night out on the town, but it seems she doesn't appreciate potpies as much as they do.

episode 6

ep 7 Treehouse

Gloria finally gets her night of salsa dancing with Jay. Cam surprises everyone when he seduces a woman on a dare. A treehouse brings neighbors together.

ep 8 After the Fire

An awkward moment on the massage table between Jay and Phil leads to greater understanding between father- and son-in-law. Alex has a band of admirers.

Episode 23

ep 9 Punkin Chunkin

What would Phil Dunphy do? A question the successful among us ask before any major decision. Manny makes a Thanksgiving "horn of ugly" centerpiece. Jay's pilaf needs more cumin, according to Manny.

ep 10 Express Christmas

Phil invents a new holiday, and the family scrambles to celebrate it.

ep 11 Lifetime Supply

When Phil runs out of his lifetime supply of razor blades, he worries it's a bad omen. Mitchell and Cam engage in an embarrassing bit of one-upmanship.

ep 12 Egg Drop

Claire and Jay compete through their respective kids' school projects. Mitchell and Cam interview prospective birth mothers.

ep 13 Little Bo Bleep

Lily's future as a flower girl is on the line as her dads try to clean up her language. Claire debates Duane Bailey in her bid for the city council spot.

ep 14 Me? Jealous?

Phil is too busy preparing dinner to notice that the prospective client he's wooing is putting the moves on Claire.

ep 15 Aunt Mommy

Jay encourages Manny to play football with the neighborhood boys. Mitchell and Cam and Claire and Phil all regret the weird plan they hatched the night before over too many drinks.

ep 16 Virgin Territory

Luke devises a trap to take Lily down a peg. Unfortunately, the cookies he uses as bait lure someone else.

episode 17

ep 17 Leap Day

Cam's birthday comes only once every four years, so the pressure's on Mitchell to host a great party.

ep 18 Send Out the Clowns

Phil gets out-agented by a smokin'-hot rival Realtor. Cam revisits his clowning days.

ep 19 Election Day

The whole family turns out for Claire, but nothing goes as planned. Walt, Luke's elderly friend, voices his opinion on Greeks.

ep 20 The Last Walt

Claire is concerned about Luke's way of dealing with the death of his friend. Phil drives fifty miles each way for a milk shake.

ep 21 Planes, Trains & Cars

Phil buys a two-seater car without consulting Claire, who is eerily calm about the whole thing.

ep 22 Disneyland

Wrangling Lily is a challenge on the family vacation.

ep 23 Tableau Vivant

Gloria's reaction to her first bite of the famous Jay Pritchett sandwich is not quite as glowing as Jay had hoped.

ep 24 Baby on Board

Manny introduces Jay to charcuterie. Alex goes to her first school dance, and Lily has a dance rehearsal.

ep 1   Bringing Up Baby

Families tend to expand, in more ways than one. Gloria has two big surprises for Jay on his birthday. Dylan moves in with the Dunphys.

ep 2   Schooled

Gloria wins the baby-swaddling race in the parenting class she's taking with Jay. Cam and Mitchell spar with the lesbian parents of a rival kid in Lily's new kindergarten.

ep 3   Snip

Phil goes under the knife. Cam completes his masterwork: a Lycra mermaid costume . . . for the cat.

episode 4

ep 4   The Butler's Escape

Cam has a new job, and Mitchell is picking up the Lily-tending duties. Luke breaks some difficult news to Phil: He wants to abandon his study of magic.

ep 5   Open House of Horrors

Maybe it's the pregnancy hormones, maybe it's because she's Colombian and her country is "covered in coffee," but Gloria's been on a rampage. By neighborhood decree, Claire is forced to rein in her Halloween decorations.

ep 6   Yard Sale

Cam and Mitchell assess Alex's new sort-of boyfriend with the age-old question: Is he, or isn't he? Gloria is oddly secretive about the contents of a mysterious trunk from Colombia.

ep 7   Arrested

Cam feeds an allergic Luke his homemade soy-based faux fakon, or fauxcon. Dede and Gloria find common ground as they reminisce about Jay's lack of interest in the whole parenting thing.

ep 8   Mistery Date

Manny and Luke crash a few bar mitzvahs and gorge on prime rib and latkes. Things get awkward when Phil has a friend over for football and Killer Margs.

ep 9   When a Tree Falls

Will Cam's obligations as an understudy in a local theater production conflict with his newfound environmental activism? Manny reluctantly attends a sports-themed birthday party.

ep 10   Diamond in the Rough

Claire makes chocolate chip pancakes for Haley's first day of work. Claire and Cam build a field of dreams, and figure it's a small leap to flipping a house; Phil and Mitchell aren't so sure.

ep 11   New Year's Eve

Jay takes the adults of the family to a—well, let's call it vintage—hotel in Palm Springs, leaving Haley and Alex—mostly Alex—in charge at home. Manny blends up his signature beverage, the Piña Delgado.

episode 12

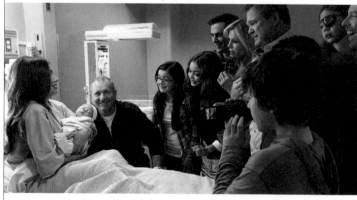

ep 12   Party Crasher

Manny's feeling neglected by Gloria, and his surprise birthday party features a surprising guest. Haley is dating a smarmy older man, a jeans designer.

episode 22

ep 13   Fulgencio

Gloria's mother and depressing sister from Colombia come to help out with the new baby. Phil steps into his role as godfather (and fixer) with ease. Cam and Mitchell are disinvited to Crispin's annual party of the century.

ep 14   A Slight at the Opera

The star of Cam Tucker's Phantom of the Opera takes ill, and Manny has a tough decision to make. Jay, Phil, Mitchell, and Pepper bond on the golf course. Alex's skepticism is challenged.

ep 15   Heart Broken

Juliana—er, Claire—has a health scare. Cam and Mitchell throw a Valentine's Day party for their single friends that's so good it's unmemorable.

ep 16   Bad Hair Day

Phil meets Claire's ex at her college reunion. Cam's so-not-clichéd Old Hollywood–themed photo shoot with Lily and Joe goes off the rails. Manny faces rejection and sees his future as a "musicless gray hellscape."

ep 17   Best Men

Mitchell and Cam's wild friend Sal announces she's getting married the next day. Phil plays Cyrano for Luke. Alex has a "cello thing" that isn't what anyone expected.

ep 18   The Wow Factor

Claire and Cam, who are renovating a house to flip, don't see eye to eye on spectacular water features. Luke trains Mitchell in the art of handball.

ep 19   The Future Dunphys

Lily decides she's gay and that pho is sometimes a bad word. Luke refines his pre-buttered toast and self-flipping pancake inventions.

ep 20   Flip Flop

Flipping a house, perhaps not surprisingly, proves to be considerably harder than flipping pancakes manually; Phil and co. resort to cyberstalking a potential buyer.

ep 21   Career Day

Phil gets shown up by Gil and his branded pickles, and Claire, fifteen years off the market, is tempted by a job offer.

ep 22   My Hero

Phil's clever mnemonic device (KALCUBO) helps Gloria learn to roller-skate. Cam is not impressed by Mitchell's charming and successful ex-boyfriend.

ep 23   Games People Play

The Dunphys are on the road in a Winnebag-no. Gloria turns out to be no good at Pictionary, but excellent at snooping. Cam's brownies are delicious.

ep 24   Goodnight, Gracie

Gloria's past catches up with her in Florida, giving Mitchell the opportunity to play Perry Mason in real life. Cam is in his element in a drama- and gossip-infested retirement community.

ep 1 Suddenly, Last Summer

Claire uses witchcraft to arrange seven kid-free days for her and Phil during summer vacation, and we learn that every couple's origin story is different and romantic in its own ways.

episode 2

ep 2 First Days

On her first day of her new job, Claire brings cookies. Big mistake. Cam's substitute teaching gig may be more than he can handle.

ep 3 Larry's Wife

Phil's recent-divorcée clients make unreasonable demands on his time. But they do make mean quick breads.

ep 4 Farm Strong

Phil's robot gutter cleaner murders a family of crows. Cam's sister Pam visits from the farm, and Cam and Mitchell dread breaking the news of their engagement.

ep 5 The Late Show

Jay pulls strings to get a reservation at a fancy new restaurant. The evening ends up at a taco truck. Claire and Phil leave Luke home alone for the first time.

ep 6 The Help

Gloria wants to hire a male nanny to help out with Joe, but Manny isn't sure about having another manny in the house.

ep 7 A Fair to Remember

Manny's entry in a cake contest is in dubious taste. He could have used Popper's help defeating Enid's "piece of sheet" cake.

ep 8 Closetcon '13

Claire and Jay attend the North American closet industry's premier trade show. Mitchell and Lily visit Cam's family on the farm in Missouri for the first time, and Cam's conservative grandmother agrees to attend their wedding. Lily becomes adept in the use of "y'all."

ep 9 The Big Game

Phil's having a tough time selling houses, but he stays upbeat. Cam scores a major victory as a high school football coach.

ep 10 The Old Man & the Tree

Gloria and Pilar make Christmas cookies. Phil has just hours to walk to Canada on his elliptical machine. Cam and Lily learn the meaning of Christmas.

ep 11 And One to Grow On

Ballroom dance class is no Autopsy Camp, but Phil is hoping Luke will get on board. Claire is frustrated by Alex's poor driving.

ep 12 Under Pressure

The parents fall into well-worn roles at the school open house. Alex opens up in therapy.

ep 13 Three Dinners

Haley has a life plan. Cam and Mitchell need some dinner-conversation starters.

episode 5

ep 14 iSpy

Luke is up to something, and Phil is determined to find out what. Phil advises Jay on how to deal with demanding women like Gloria and Claire.

ep 15 The Feud

Luke competes against the son of Phil's archenemy, Gil Thorpe, in a wrestling match. A lice outbreak in Lily's class threatens Cam and Mitchell's appointment with an in-demand wedding photographer.

ep 16 Spring-a-Ding-Fling

Phil hosts the annual Realtors' banquet. A beloved Spanish teacher returns from sabbatical and steals Cam's thunder.

ep 17 Other People's Children

Phil reveals his secret to great banana bread, and Jay teaches Luke some manly life skills.

ep 18 Las Vegas

Claire and Phil have different agendas on a trip to Sin City. Hers does not involve a meeting of a secret underground society of magicians. Cam is more interested in the Kilty Pleasures floor show than he lets on to Mitchell.

ep 19 A Hard Jay's Night

Cam's dad sends a well-executed but horrendous and possibly offensive wedding gift.

ep 20 Australia

Phil returns to the country of his conception and brings the whole family along. Unfortunately, Australia

is unkind to him—a series of mishaps ensue.

ep 21 Sleeper

A Carly Simon ballad brings back memories for Phil. Jay demonstrates that he knows his pup Stella better than he knows his own son.

ep 22 Message Received

Jay and Manny step out of their comfort zones. Manny eats a pickle; Jay eats blood sausage.

episode 20

ep 23 The Wedding, Part 1

As the clock ticks and a natural disaster looms, last-minute wedding preparations suffer some setbacks.

ep 24 The Wedding, Part 2

After a series of changes in plans, Phil steps in to officiate Cam and Mitchell's long-awaited wedding.

episode 22

episode 4

ep 1 The Long Honeymoon

It's been a perfect summer at the Dunphy household—until Alex returns from a stint with Habitat for Humanity.

ep 2 Do Not Push

Alex is college shopping. Cam and Mitchell's attempts to shoot a family portrait are thwarted by Lily's inability to make a non-terrifying facial expression.

ep 3 The Cold

Wedding video evidence implicates Phil as a disease vector. Mitchell struggles with the idea that Lily might not be as precocious as one of her friends.

ep 4 Marco Polo

Phil wants to spend time with his family. Is sport-phobic Mitchell's "bad energy" jinxing Coach Cam's football team?

ep 5 Won't You Be Our Neighbor

Phil's adherence to the Realtor code of ethics is tested when terrible people want to buy the house next door.

ep 6 Halloween 3: AwesomeLand

Phil's sunny vision for this year's Halloween theme conflicts with Claire's über-morbid approach to her favorite holiday.

ep 7 Queer Eyes, Full Hearts

Gloria hires a handsome Spanish tutor for Manny. Cam is a natural as the subject of a journalist's human-interest story.

ep 8 Three Turkeys

With Phil and Luke cooking Thanksgiving dinner, Claire decides to prepare a secret backup turkey.

ep 9 Strangers in the Night

Once again, Alex's boyfriend invites questions. This time, though, it's whether he exists at all.

ep 10 Haley's 21st Birthday

Gloria is enthusiastic about Haley getting a tattoo—a big one.

ep 11 The Day We Almost Died

Each person reacts differently to a near-death experience.

ep 12 The Big Guns

Phil and Claire's plans to give their tacky neighbors a taste of their own medicine backfire. Cam wants to raise Lily as a clown.

ep 13 Rash Decisions

As Luke begins to distance himself from his father, Phil starts spending more time with Andy. Gloria thinks there needs to be more distance between baby Joe and Stella.

ep 14 Valentine's Day 4: Twisted Sister

Phil breaks up with Juliana. Gloria's grim and slightly disturbed sister comes between her and Jay.

episode 6

episode 14

ep 15 Fight or Flight

Sal, a new mother, seems to have changed her party-girl ways. Manny deals with a bully in his cooking class—on lasagna day.

ep 16 Connection Lost

Haley is missing and presumed pregnant and married, but through online stalking, texts, and video chats, Claire tracks her down.

ep 17 Closet? You'll Love It!

For the good of the company, Claire is forced to enter into delicate negotiations with her boss.

ep 18 Spring Break

Haley takes Alex to a music festival to take her mind off college applications—and everything else.

ep 19 Grill, Interrupted

Phil's fancy birthday gift to Jay backfires—almost literally. Alex has second thoughts about her choice of college. Luke and Manny learn an important lesson about drinking.

ep 20 Knock 'Em Down

Claire and Phil learn that their tacky neighbors, like fine wines, contain unimagined depths. Jay does Cam a favor and finds himself at the center of a gay-bowling-league controversy. Gloria and Mitchell plan on a night of clubbing with Haley, but have a hard time keeping up.

ep 21 Integrity

Jay and Phil find common ground as they kvetch about their

respective wives. Mitchell and Cam are again thinking about adopting another baby. Claire stoops to bribery in an attempt to secure a school award for Luke.

ep 22 Patriot Games

Mitchell and Cam's political loyalties are tested when they join a

episode 13

protest against a restaurant they secretly really want to try. Alex is horrified that her nemesis, Sanjay, is going to share her title as valedictorian.

ep 23 Crying Out Loud

Claire faces an existential crisis when she's offered a job with a big hotel chain. Manny has his wisdom teeth pulled, and his drugged-up state leaves him at the mercy of his mother.

ep 24 American Skyper

Alex is graduating! And Phil is stuck in Seattle—but he devises an ingenious way to be at the ceremony anyway. Andy's girlfriend, Beth, is visiting from out of town, and tensions with Haley reach a tipping point.

index

photo credits